MEANINGFUL COINCIDENCES

"Synchronicity connects you with nonlocal awareness and with others. Serendipity is opportunity meets preparedness. This book is an excellent guide."

DEEPAK CHOPRA, M.D.

"A pioneering work—Beitman synthesizes findings from diverse disciplines, ranging from theology to biogeochemistry, which are as convincing as they are awe-inspiring. Dr. Beitman expands our understanding of uncanny coincidence by applying his discriminating eye as a former academic researcher and his receptive heart and spirit as a psychiatrist in private practice who engages in these lived mysteries with his patients. Upon reading, expect to experience more meaningful coincidences."

HELEN MARLO, PH.D., PROFESSOR OF CLINICAL PSYCHOLOGY AND THE DEPARTMENT CHAIR AT NOTRE DAME DE NAMUR UNIVERSITY

"Is it a mere coincidence that you've noticed this book on coincidences? After you've read it, you may agree with author and psychiatrist Bernard Beitman that some synchronicities are far more than dumb luck. They also provide clues about the holistic fabric of reality that binds everything and everyone together. A thoroughly engaging and well-written examination of a perpetually fascinating form of human experience."

DEAN RADIN, PH.D., CHIEF SCIENTIST AT THE INSTITUTE OF NOETIC SCIENCES

"Bernard Beitman has given us something fundamentally new and helpful here: a careful and rigorous modeling of coincidences that are not just coincidences and then a way of practically integrating them into our lives, thought, and public culture. Many writers have commented on the subject. None have been this careful, this thorough, and, frankly, this eloquent. If I may, Dr. Beitman makes the impossible possible. Welcome to the psychosphere."

JEFFREY J. KRIPAL, PH.D., AUTHOR OF *THE SUPERHUMANITIES*

"In *Meaningful Coincidences,* Dr. Beitman argues that meaningful coincidences are both common and normal in everyday life. Brimming with astounding examples, this important book introduces a typology of coincidences that brings much-needed conceptual rigor to their study and understanding. Beitman shows how, regardless of their cause or mechanism, we can use meaningful coincidences to enrich our lives and help heal our fractured society. This book will challenge what you thought you knew about your life and role in the world."

BRUCE GREYSON, M.D., CHESTER F. CARLSON PROFESSOR EMERITUS
OF PSYCHIATRY AND NEUROBEHAVIORAL SCIENCES,
UNIVERSITY OF VIRGINIA

"In this fascinating analysis of the anatomy of coincidences, the author dives into what makes coincidences meaningful and what we can learn from them. If you'd like to explore this exciting topic—and learn how to open yourself up to meaningful coincidences—this book is for you."

CHRISTIAN BUSCH, PH.D., CLINICAL ASSISTANT PROFESSOR
AT NYU AND AUTHOR OF *THE SERENDIPITY MINDSET*

"A wonderful, highly readable account of meaningful coincidences. The author—a psychiatrist, researcher, podcast host, and more—has devoted considerable talent, time, and resources to legitimizing the study of coincidences. His systemic categorizations of these types of events along with the articulation of coincidence sensitivity and discussions of meta-coincidence make this a uniquely valuable contribution to anyone seriously interested in the field."

JOSEPH CAMBRAY, PH.D., PRESIDENT-CEO OF
PACIFICA GRADUATE INSTITUTE

"This book is a transdisciplinary look into the nature of connection itself. In tracing the mechanisms and mysteries of coincidence and charting the paradoxical nature of its exploration (for to discover the reason behind a coincidence is to render it no longer one), Beitman delightfully reveals that there is room for data in awe—but also room for awe in data."

A. NATASHA JOUKOVSKY, AUTHOR OF *THE PORTRAIT OF A MIRROR*

"I have known Dr. Beitman as an earnest and dogged investigator of what lies beneath the wonder of synchronicity experienced by so many. He goes further than pursuing knowledge about these phenomena for its own sake, however. He has founded a community of fellows who share his drive, drawing from shared wisdom, and thus Beitman's work represents a growing body of data on personal experiences in and around phenomena such as synchronicity and serendipity."

SAMANTHA COPELAND, PH.D., PHILOSOPHER AND COFOUNDER
AND COCHAIR OF THE SERENDIPITY SOCIETY

MEANINGFUL COINCIDENCES

How and Why Synchronicity and Serendipity Happen

A Sacred Planet Book

BERNARD BEITMAN, M.D.

Park Street Press
Rochester, Vermont

Park Street Press
One Park Street
Rochester, Vermont 05767
www.ParkStPress.com

Text stock is SFI certified

Park Street Press is a division of Inner Traditions International

Sacred Planet Books are curated by Richard Grossinger, Inner Traditions editorial board member and cofounder and former publisher of North Atlantic Books. The Sacred Planet collection, published under the umbrella of the Inner Traditions family of imprints, includes works on the themes of consciousness, cosmology, alternative medicine, dreams, climate, permaculture, alchemy, shamanic studies, oracles, astrology, crystals, hyperobjects, locutions, and subtle bodies.

Cataloging-in-Publication Data for this title is available from the Library of Congress

ISBN 978-1-64411-570-1 (print)
ISBN 978-1-64411-571-8 (ebook)

Printed and bound in the United States by Lake Book Manufacturing, Inc. The text stock is SFI certified. The Sustainable Forestry Initiative® program promotes sustainable forest management.

10 9 8 7 6 5 4 3 2 1

Text design and layout by Kenleigh Manseau
This book was typeset in Garamond Premier Pro with Futura, Gill Sans, GriffithGothic, and Legacy Sans

To send correspondence to the author of this book, mail a first-class letter to the author c/o Inner Traditions • Bear & Company, One Park Street, Rochester, VT 05767, and we will forward the communication, or contact the author directly at **coincider.com**.

Dedicated to the seeds of this book:
Snapper and Karl Beitman
of blessed memory

Contents

PART 3

Incorporating Coincidence
into Your Life

The Invisible Currents That Connect and Unite Us

Terry Marks-Tarlow, Ph.D.

Bernard Beitman, M.D., has experienced and studied coincidences for decades. This book emerged from his infectious passion and extensive scholarship and may be the most comprehensive guidebook ever written on the subject. He examines coincidences through multiple lenses—Carl Jung's "synchronicity" (meaningful coincidences), Horace Walpole's "serendipity" (happy accidents), Paul Kammerer's "seriality" (recurrence of numbers or events), and his own concept of "simulpathity" (empathic resonances across space or time). He also systematically categorizes coincidences into three types, explains the conditions likely to stimulate them, describes their benefits as well as limitations, and illuminates the spectrum of possible explanations.

Dr. Beitman describes the range of patterns by which people experience coincidences. These include: generalists, connectors, super-encounterers, serialiers, probabilists, and theoreticians. I am a "generalist" insofar as coincidences of all kinds have always been central to my life. When younger, I recall special delight in grabbing a handful of nails, only to discover I had nabbed *exactly* the number I needed. In my role as a clinical psychologist, coincidences appear regularly. They show up as clusters in new patients, like a series of artists or a series of attorneys. They emerge from patient stories when outer events perfectly mirror inner issues. The deeper or more charged the subject matter, the more likely synchronicities are to appear. Both personally and professionally, these occurrences continually inform me whether I am "in the flow" or facing a block.

Some people draw upon normative statistics that, by themselves, render coincidences meaningless. By contrast, contemporary math and science offer alternate possibilities. As Dr. Beitman states, Jung was influenced by the physicist Wolfgang Pauli, a patient of his who introduced him to the concept of nonlocality, the ability of quantum particles to become instantly entangled even across huge expanses of space. I too am steeped in contemporary science, which informs not only my view of synchronicity but also my spirituality. I hold a special love for fractal geometry, a passion shared by Rob Sacco and explained in the pages ahead. I believe that fractals constitute a meta-level of patterns in the universe—the patterns of the patterns we see.

Fractal geometry is a new branch of mathematics, dating back to the 1970s. From the field's inception, discoverer/inventor Benoît Mandelbrot recognized the relevance of fractals for capturing very complicated natural shapes. The hallmark of a fractal, self-similarity, means that the pattern of the whole is reflected in the pattern of the parts. We see this in the branching fractals of trees, rivers, the arteries of our bodies, and neurons, in all natural landscapes like coastlines and mountains, and, at a cultural level, within archetypes found worldwide like the Trickster, Shadow, Good Mother, and Hero that are repeated throughout human history.

Dr. Beitman intuitively understood the connection between fractals and meaningful coincidences when he chose a fractal spiral to grace the cover of this book. The author and I met through an interview on his podcast *Connecting with Coincidence* (episode 239) after I had served as lead editor for the book *A Fractal Epistemology for a Scientific Psychology*. During our talk, I claimed that fractal principles provide the best naturalistic model of how mind and matter so frequently mirror one another.

Self-similar patterns occur across multiple scales, whether in space or time or across imaginary, symbolic realms. Self-similar spirals recur in the growth of a nautilus shell and some snails, the pattern of a sunflower's seeds, or a galaxy's curve. As the snail grows, the shell's curve retains the same relationship between part and whole. This is the essence of identity everywhere—though our parts may change, they retain a vital relationship to the whole: I am still myself, even though all the cells and fluids in my body or the ideas in my mind continually change.

Fractal patterns also hold surprises, such as the closer you look, the more self-similar pattern there is to see. Fractals also sport paradoxical boundaries that are simultaneously open and closed. I may function autonomously in some ways, yet I have a social brain that continually penetrates and is penetrated by others. Interpersonal fractals may help to explain interpersonal resonances.

After our interview Dr. Beitman entered a twilight zone between sleep and waking that prompted him to invite me to write this foreword. Since then he's been seeing fractals everywhere, while I have been besieged by coincidences. This is an example of relational interpenetration. We may leave the womb, but our relationship with the whole never falters—we interpenetrate with others and with our environment. With mind and matter conceived this way, we can view coincidences naturalistically in terms of self-similar resonances between inner and outer processes. Like tuning forks, our brains, minds, and bodies sync up with one another as well as with nature at large.

Dear reader, you will enjoy the pages ahead. Not only are they filled with fascinating examples of coincidences they also illustrate a variety of ways to understand, categorize, and ascribe meaning to such events. Coincidences cannot help but fill us with wonder at the fundamental interconnection between inner and outer realms.

Your personal synchronicities are both astounding yet common events. Dr. Beitman's book will help you normalize your experience of them and empower you to feel more confident in telling your relatives and friends about them. If you are as moved by what you read as I was, I hope you will join Dr. Beitman in collectively using meaning-ful coincidences to illuminate the invisible currents that connect and unite us.

Terry Marks-Tarlow, Ph.D., is the editor of *A Fractal Epistemology for a Scientific Psychology* (2020) as well as the author of *Mythic Imagination Today: The Interpenetration of Mythology and Science* (2021).

How Coincidence Shaped My Life

The greatest thing you'll ever learn
is just to love and be loved in return.
"Nature Boy," Nat King Cole

Please allow me to introduce myself. I am a psychiatrist. I am paid to distinguish between reality and crazy. I walk that line in my life and in this book.

A meaningful coincidence is the coming together of two or more events in a surprising, unexpected, and improbable way that seems to have significance to the person experiencing it, either at the moment or in retrospect.

Coincidences have been a regular companion throughout my life beginning at age nine when my dog got lost, and I got lost. Then we found each other. Coincidences were deeply solidified in my consciousness when, at age thirty-one, I found myself uncontrollably choking while, three thousand miles away, my father was choking on his own blood and dying.

The experiences of meaningful coincidences have expanded my awareness of my mind and heart, of the heart and mind of others, and of the natural world around us. Coincidences have contributed to my psychological and spiritual development, guided me in my academic career, and helped grow my relationships. They have jolted me out of the conventional views of how the world works. They have made me stop, think, and wonder.

In high school, I imagined hitting the first pitch of the game for a homerun. I did it once. In college, I imagined running the opening kickoff back for a touchdown. I did it once. What did imagining have to do with the actual events? Were they "just a coincidence?"

I went to Yale Medical School and completed a psychiatric residency at Stanford. My richest coincidence environment was San Francisco's Haight-Ashbury district in the late 1960s. I was a part-time psychiatric resident and part-time hippie, spending half the week at Stanford and half the week on the streets of the city. During those days, coincidences flew rapidly into my consciousness.

Shortly before I left the University of Washington for a faculty position at the University of Missouri in Columbia, Missouri, a coincidence presented me a promising research direction. When I walked into a colleague's office to say goodbye to him and the work we had done together, I noticed a paper on chest pain and panic disorder on his desk. Noticing my interest, he presented me with a one-page protocol, which I then took to Missouri. When I arrived at the University of Missouri, I found that the back door of the cardiology clinic was directly across the hall from the front door of the psychiatry clinic, allowing for easy, confidential movement of chest pain patients to the psychiatric interviews I would conduct. Coincidence!

I would end up publishing more than forty papers on the subject, which fostered my being promoted to chairman of the department of psychiatry, where I developed an innovative training program in the basics of psychotherapy for psychiatric residents, and for which I received two national awards. My superb research assistant was a Chinese psychiatrist whom I had met on a speaking tour at China Medical University in Shenyang. How conveniently coincidental!

By 2006, I had established my credentials as a successful academic psychiatrist, so I could return to my passion for coincidences. Building on my research experiences in chest pain and my work on psychotherapy, I could formally ask to what degree people experience what kind of coincidences. I hired psychology graduate students to help quantify answers to that question.

Through a series of standard iterations, we developed the Weird Coincidence Survey (WCS). We ran two separate studies involving approximately one thousand volunteers from the university faculty, staff, and students and published the results in two issues of *Psychiatric Annals.* As editor of each issue, I recruited other synchronicity authors to contribute articles. For the second edition, three research teams from three other universities reported the results of their studies using the WCS. The WCS has been on my website since 2016 for anyone to take to get an estimate of their sensitivity to coincidences. By the end of 2020 more than 2,600 people had taken the survey, which offered us the opportunity to elaborate on earlier findings.

I left the University of Missouri for Charlottesville, Virginia, where I became a visiting professor in the department of psychiatry and neurobehavioral sciences at the University of Virginia. As a private practitioner and "recovering academic," I wrote *Connecting with Coincidence,* my first book on the subject, which organized a large collection of coincidence stories by their impacts on, and usefulness in, key aspects of daily life: romance, family, friends, health, jobs, ideas, money, and spirituality. I began writing a *Psychology Today* blog, which by 2021 had more than 100 entries with more than 750,000 reads, and I produced a radio show with 138 episodes and more than 250,000 downloads. I then began a zoom-based podcast in which I interviewed guests from a wide spectrum of life experiences. Coincidences are part of life's flow wherever you are.

The radio show and podcast allowed me to have illuminating conversations with leaders in the study of coincidences including Jungians, statisticians, entrepreneurs, serendipity academics, musicians, people with bipolar disorder, parapsychologists, naturalists, religious fundamentalists, shamans, and people whose coincidence experiences moved them to write books about synchronicity. Some of these interviewees are featured in *Meaningful Coincidences*. The radio show *Connecting with Coincidence* can be found on Spreaker and YouTube at youtube .com/c/Coinciders/videos as well as on my website coincider.com.

In September 2019 I presented an introduction to meaningful coincidences at the first meeting of the Serendipity Society, an exciting and determined group of academics who are bringing the formal study of coincidences to universities in Europe, North America, and Asia.

This book brings much needed scholarship to the study of coincidences. It presents the first systematic categorization of meaningful coincidences. Unlike all previous contributions, this book describes the anatomy of a coincidence, an extensive survey of the different types of coincidences, the conditions that increase the likelihood of their occurring, their limitations as well as benefits, and the wide variety of hypotheses that have been put forward to explain them.

The primary intent of this book is to serve as a guide to anyone wishing to incorporate the flow of coincidences in their life. For those deeply interested in the subject, this book encourages you to join us in The Coincidence Project, which is described in appendix 1.

Meaningful Coincidences is also intended to interest academics to study them and to accelerate the telling of coincidence stories in everyday conversations. The richest source for the evolution of coincidence studies comes from reports by people living their lives. By encouraging both academic interest and storytelling in daily life, this book can create bridges between researchers and the people experiencing coincidences.

As an academic psychiatrist, I have been paid well to serve others both financially and experientially. I want to repay society's generosity. This report of what I've learned about coincidences is the product of my gratitude. May it assist in the positive evolution of our human mind and spirit.

PART I

Defining
Coincidence

1

Anatomy of a Coincidence

The words *coincide* and *coincidence* came into English through philosophy, likely from translations from the Latin of Roger Bacon (1220–1292). The words then passed into the vocabulary of scholarly English writers during the first half of the seventeenth century and then were taken up by mathematicians during the great revival of mathematical study at that time in England.

The word *coincidence* became a household word in American English following the simultaneous deaths of Thomas Jefferson and John Adams on July 4, 1826. The pair died exactly fifty years after each had signed the United States Declaration of Independence.[1]

So then, what is a coincidence? We actually know very little about what they are. That reality is best illustrated by the dictionary definition, which states that a coincidence is the remarkable concurrence of events or circumstances without apparent causal connection. Why is it remarkable? Because they occur at the same time? Because their concurrence is surprising? Because there is no apparent cause though it seems there should be one? And left unsaid in that definition is the suggestion that the coincidence may have meaning.

The definition of coincidence harbors contradictions. There could be no cause or there could be a cause. It could have no meaning or could be meaningful. Coincidences may be both improbable and surprising, but these are not synonyms. Coincidences tend to be improbable events, but all improbable events aren't necessarily coincidences.[2] For example, rolling a die six times and getting 464255 might be just as improbable as 666666, but not nearly as surprising.[3] Similarly, coincidences are usually surprising.[4] But events that are surprising (e.g., an unexpected firecracker or birthday party) are not necessarily coincidences.[5,6] So a surprising and improbable coincidence captures attention and seems to demand explanation.

Our attempt to understand what is meant by the word *coincidence* is made all the more difficult at the starting gate because the word *coincidence* is used in two starkly opposing ways: either as attention-worthy or as irrelevant. Adjectives used with the word *coincidence* sharpen the direction of the intended meaning. When coincidences are thought to be important or to have a cause, whatever it may be, the speaker will use adjectives such as meaningful, remarkable, or amazing. "That was an amazing coincidence," one might say. When the coincidence is viewed as irrelevant, as due to chance, adjectives such as mere, only, pure, sheer, and just will modify the word. "That's just a coincidence." And when the word is used without a modifying adjective, the speaker's intended meaning may be unclear: "It was a coincidence that you showed up when I did."

But one thing about coincidences is certain: they are all around us. In our daily lives, on the internet, radio, and television, and in our entertainment; but like the gorilla in the room, we often don't notice them, or do so only briefly, in passing, and often without giving them a second thought. The survey I conducted while at the University of Missouri in 2009 found that at least a third of the general population frequently notices coincidences.[7] That's a good start and suggests to me that perhaps it's time to create a new field to explore how these unexpected conjunctions of events can be understood. To this end, I have established the nonprofit organization called The Coincidence Project, which includes the transdisciplinary field of coincidence studies (see appendix 1 for more on this). But first, let's begin by pulling apart the threads of what's commonly called a coincidence.

TIMELINESS

When we consider coincidences, what variables are involved? The first and most obvious one is the time interval. Coincidences are commonly viewed as the coming together of two or more events simultaneously in time, or nearly so. The instantaneous or short time interval between the coincidental events seems to increase the significance of a coincidence in peoples' minds, because short time intervals between the occurrences of two seemingly unrelated events begin to suggest a cause. Lightning is quickly followed by thunder, so lightning causes thunder.

But, in fact, the time intervals characterizing coinciding events can vary from simultaneous to many years. And coincidental events taking place years apart can be every bit as astonishing as those that are instantaneous. Take this example as related by psychologist Alan Combs and English professor Mark Holland in their book *Synchronicity: Through the Eyes of Science, Myth and the Trickster:* "Allen Falby was a highway patrolman in Texas. One night on duty he crashed his motorcycle and lay bleeding to death on the road, having ruptured a major artery in his leg. At that point, a man named Alfred Smith arrived, quickly put a tourniquet on his leg, and saved his life. Five years later, Falby was again on duty and received a call to go to the scene of an auto accident. There, he found a man who was bleeding to death from a severed artery in his leg. He applied a tourniquet and saved the man's life. Only then did he find out it was Alfred Smith, the very man who had saved his life in the exact same way five years earlier. Falby joked, 'It all goes to prove that one good tourniquet deserves another.'"[8]

In the creation of a coincidence, time is generally viewed as going forward: a person thinks of something and then an event or object in the environment matches that thought. But as the Allen Falby story illustrates, coincidences can also be recognized by looking back in time and matching events retrospectively.

SIMILARITY

Another variable in coincidences is similarity: the two or more events making up a coincidence must be similar. In the Allen Falby example, both events involve a tourniquet on the leg saving the life of a man bleeding to death. That in itself is not a coincidence, but the fact the two men happen to save each other's lives years apart without knowing or being involved with one another—and each showing up at the right place and time to save the other person's life—is what makes it a meaningful coincidence.

It would be seen as somewhat less of a coincidence if Falby, who had been saved from bleeding to death with a tourniquet applied by Smith, had saved Smith say, from drowning, by resuscitation. And perhaps it would not be seen as a coincidence at all if they were both in the same police department; that would certainly be the case if they were patrol partners.

IMPROBABILITY

Similarity brings up the subject of statistical probability, a subject we will deal with in greater detail in a subsequent chapter 5. But as another variable of coincidences, it is also discussed briefly here. Though not stated explicitly in the dictionary definition of coincidence, it's understood that a coincidence is an unlikely event. Finding your watch in the pocket of a coat you haven't worn for months is not a coincidence. It's forgetfulness. Thinking of your mother just as your mother happens to call you is not a coincidence, or at least not an unlikely one. After all, she is your mother, you probably think of her often, and she does call you from time to time.

The higher the probability of a coincidence, the more likely there is a conventional explanation for the coincidence. But the lower the probability (or the higher the improbability) of a coincidence, the less likely simple mathematical randomness can explain the concurrence, and the more likely that the cause or explanation for the coincidence lies outside the realm of conventional science.

Improbability is related to the degree of surprise of a coincidence. The less likely it is, the more surprising it will be. One of your friends arriving on time for coffee does not qualify as a coincidence. It is not surprising, though you may be glad to see your friend. There must be some element in the intersection of two events that makes it surprising. Surprising coincidences make us wonder. They stretch our sense of what's normal, what's probable.

Along with its improbability, the degree of surprise of an event is evaluated according to its relevance: How directly does the combination of coinciding events relate to the moment? If you were thinking about the origin of the moon, and as you walk through the library a book on raising a baby falls on your foot, you likely wouldn't think twice about it. But what if the subject of the book that falls on your foot is the moon? When the coincidence seems to provide a comment on a current set of thoughts, the sense of surprise is amplified.

The degree to which a coincidence is surprising helps determine how much we will pay attention to it. Without some surprise we would not look any further at the parallel; we would not search for its significance or meaning. It's the surprise element that moves us to look further.

THE TWO PRIMARY MEANINGS OF MEANINGFUL COINCIDENCES

When experiencing a coincidence, the *coincider,* the person experiencing a coincidence, often asks, "What does this mean?" Within this question are embedded two different questions. One question is "How did this happen?" The answer becomes an explanation. The other question is "What does this mean for me?" This answer becomes possible guidance for how to use the coincidence. (The ranges of explanations and uses are described later in this book.)

THE MOST COMMON FORMS
OF COINCIDENCE

David Spiegelhalter, the Winton professor for the public understanding of risk at the University of Cambridge, collected more than 4,470 coincidences. The text analytics firm Quid then did an analysis of those stories. A solid 58 percent of the coincidences "included words related to family or loved ones, indicating that people are more likely to notice coincidences involving people closest to them."

The five most common types of coincidences in this analysis were:

1. Sharing a birthday with someone (11 percent)
2. Connections involving books, TV, radio, or the news (10 percent)
3. Vacation-related coincidences (6.1 percent)
4. Meeting people in transit—while walking around, in airports, or on public transportation (6 percent)
5. Coincidences related to marriage or in-laws (5.3 percent)

The researchers also looked at the tone of the stories and found that more people described their coincidences using negative language (32 percent) or neutral language (41 percent) than positive language (25 percent). This finding is unexpected because coincidences are generally considered to be positive experiences. Maybe it's because people seeking meaning are more likely to experience coincidences, and that often happens in times of distress.[9]

The WCS I conducted, beginning at the University of Missouri, approached the question in a different way. While Spiegelhalter asked participants to report their stories, WCS participants rated how often they experienced the most common coincidences on my website coincider.com. By October 13, 2020, a total of 2,612 people had answered questions on the WCS website. On a scale of 1 to 5, where 5 is "Very frequently" the most common coincidences were:

- After experiencing a meaningful coincidence, I analyze the meaning of my experience [4.04 average of responses];
- I think of an idea and hear or see it on the radio, TV, or internet [3.47];
- I think of calling someone, only to have that person unexpectedly call me [3.38];
- I advance in my work/career/education by being in the right place at the right time [3.37]; and
- I think of a question only to have it answered by an external source (i.e., radio, TV, or other people) before I can ask it [3.32].

The other coincidences, in descending order of frequency, were:

- I am introduced to people who unexpectedly further my work/career [3.19];
- I need something, and the need is then met without my having to do anything [3.19];
- I run into a friend in an out-of-the-way place [3.09];
- Meaningful coincidence helps determine my educational path [2.95];
- I think about someone and then that person unexpectedly drops by my house or office, or passes me in the hall or street [2.86];
- I experience strong emotions or physical sensations that were simultaneously experienced at a distance by someone I love [2.85]; and
- When my phone rings, I know who is calling without checking the screen or using personalized ring tones [2.80].

The participants were also ranked by coincidence sensitivity ranging from above forty-three to nineteen and below by adding their scores for each of the items on the survey.

Half the participants scored in the very sensitive and ultrasensitive range. Most likely, those people highly interested in coincidences decided to fill out the survey.

Answer Choices	Responses by Percent	Number of Responders
Above 43: Ultra Sensitive	29.20%	762
39–43: Very Sensitive	20.92%	546
35–38: Sensitive	15.82%	413
27–34: Average	21.80%	569
23–26: Somewhat Closed	6.63%	173
22–19: Closed	3.22%	84
19 and below: Ultra Closed	2.41%	63
Total	100%	2610

In both my analysis and the analysis of stories submitted to Spiegelhalter, coincidences involving media are relatively common. Though there are some similarities, it is interesting that some different categories grew out of the two different approaches. I developed my categories through an extensive literature review and statistical winnowing. Quid analyzed the content of voluntarily submitted stories to develop its categories. The Quid analysis included categories of marriage- and hospital-related coincidences, which I did not include in my survey. I included categories Quid did not, such as coincidences related to careers and the reflection of one's thoughts in the external environment. As we develop the science of coincidence studies, which is explained in more detail in appendix 1, ongoing data analyses like these will sharpen the categorization of coincidences.

2
Types of Coincidence

Words are created to carve out portions of reality that deserve our attention. The phrase *meaningful coincidence* is actually an umbrella term that covers four words used to describe various types of meaningful coincidence: Carl Jung's *synchronicity*, Horace Walpole's *serendipity*, Paul Kammerer's *seriality*, and *simulpathity*, a term I coined myself. The definitions of these four words overlap.

SYNCHRONICITY

The Swiss psychiatrist and founder of analytical psychology Carl Jung is single-handedly responsible for the emergence of the idea of meaningful coincidences in Western thought. He did so by inventing the word *synchronicity* from the Greek *syn*—"with, together"—and *chronos*—"time (as in chronology)." *Synchronicity*, then, means "together-in-time." In his writing, Jung referred to the synchronicity principle, with which he attempted to explain a variety of phenomena in addition to meaningful coincidences. For Jung, synchronicity was an acausal connecting principle by which apparently chance events were connected not by cause but by their similarity in meaning.[1] As the use of the word has evolved, it has come to be seen as the equivalent of meaningful coincidence. For single events Jung usually used the terms *coincidence* and *meaningful coincidence*. Currently synchronicity is regarded as one type of meaningful coincidence.

Jung used findings from quantum mechanics and psi research to hypothesize that synchronicity functioned outside the conventional causal reliance on time and space. He was strongly influenced by the psi experiments of J. B. Rhine at Duke University.[2] Jung's two primary examples of meaningful coincidences included clairvoyance and precognition.[3] These primary examples of the synchronicity principle have faded from the writings of his followers and have been replaced by less controversial ideas. Physicist Victor Mansfield, for example, attempted to dissociate synchronicity from the paranormal.[4] Through his towering intellect, reflected in his theoretical writings and anecdotes, Jung laid the groundwork for the twenty-first century study of meaningful coincidences.

Jung participated in the creation of the world's most famous meaningful coincidence during a therapy session. In his office in Zurich, Switzerland, he had been treating a young woman of high education and serious demeanor. But Jung could see that her quest for psychological change was doomed unless he could succeed in softening her rationalist shell. As he remained attentive to the young woman, he hoped something unexpected and irrational would turn up. And as she described a golden scarab—a costly piece of jewelry—she had received in a dream the night before, he heard a tapping on the window. Jung opened the window and plucked a scarab beetle out of the air. The beetle, closely resembling the golden scarab, was just what he needed— or just what she needed. "Here is your scarab," he said to the woman, as he handed her a link between her dream and external reality.

Jung saw this coincidence as a way of achieving his therapeutic goal, breaking through his patient's excessive rationality. "In Jung's view," notes Jungian scholar Roderick Main, "the synchronicity does what he himself could not do, but what he knew needed to be done."[5]

Jung declared that the coincidence broke down the patient's resistance, and treatment could be continued with satisfactory results. He gave no further details of the treatment or its results. The implication is that this one intervention made everything go smoothly. This idealization of the therapeutic process is more fairy tale than real world. The "how" of this magical effect is not explained. Through coincidence studies, we may come to understand this "how" more clearly.

Jung was watchful, expectant. "This state of hope for the unexpected on Jung's part," Main said, "forms the inner, psychic component of the synchronicity for him, the outer, physical component of which is the actual 'something unexpected and irrational' in the form of the scarabaeid beetle."[6] The scarab beetle was then a double synchronicity fulfilling both the patient's and Jung's need.

Jung was a conduit for the scarab coincidence. Had he not opened the window and let the beetle in, the connection might never have been made between the woman's inner and outer worlds. The scarab beetle also had significance for Jung as an Egyptian symbol of death and transformation, an archetype. It had appeared previously as a symbol in his own visions. Perhaps this added to his instrumental role in creating the coincidence. Jung believed that activating or "constellating" an archetype was necessary to create a meaningful coincidence.

Jung's scarab story remains the archetypal synchronicity—the most written about meaningful coincidence in the history of coincidence studies. Just as Jung was instrumental in bringing about the coincidence of the scarab beetle, he was instrumental in bringing the idea of synchronicity to the world. Synchronicity is to the Western world like the golden scarab was to Jung's patient, something he handed us with an air of great mystery, with fairy tale magic that challenges our views of causality.[7]

Therapists continue to use coincidence in their work. Psychologist Frank Pasciuti describes a similar coincidence. Just as he was urging a reluctant patient to consult a specific psychologist for a formal evaluation of possible ADHD, a woman burst into his office asking if this was the office of the very same psychologist he was recommending to his patient. Like Jung's patient, Frank's patient took the hint and finally agreed to see that psychologist. The patient was evaluated and was diagnosed with severe ADHD.

For his part, Main has committed himself to the careful study of

Jung's approach to synchronicity. "I have been researching coincidence for over 25 years," writes Main, "focusing mostly on Carl Jung's seminal concept of synchronicity. Jung's approach appeals to me because of his openness to the full range of coincidence phenomena, even those that involve seemingly paranormal elements. I like that Jung, while not disregarding issues of proof and explanation, focuses primarily on what coincidences and other anomalous phenomena mean—and the range of meanings he recognizes can stretch from the mundane to the cosmic. I also like his boldness in allowing his psychological theories, as well as his view of reality, to be shaped by the phenomena he encountered, and not vice versa."[8]

Jung placed his acausal connecting principle on equal status with causation. It differs from causality by being independent of time and space.[9] In its simplest form, *acausal* means that figuring out how A caused B is difficult to determine. Sometimes it's even hard to know which came first, A or B. For Jung, a shared meaning, via an activated archetype, connects the two events. Jung's arguments for acausality have several weaknesses.[10] The primary value of these arguments is to shift attention away from causality to meaning as the connecting principle between the elements of a meaningful coincidence.[11]

Those who follow Jung maintain that synchronicity, true synchronicities, are only those coincidences that serve the quest for self-realization, for personal and spiritual growth, and for a deeper experience of human interconnectedness.[12,13]

SERENDIPITY

Horace Walpole, a member of the British House of Commons in the eighteenth century, recognized in himself a talent for finding what he needed just when he needed it. Walpole first coined the term for this talent in a letter to his friend and distant cousin Horace Mann, the British minister in Florence, Italy. Mann had sent Walpole a portrait of the Grand Duchess Bianco Capello whom Walpole had long admired.

Walpole wanted to frame it with the coat of arms from the Capello family, and not long after he just happened to find the needed coat of arms in an old book he had picked up. On January 28, 1754, thrilled with this coincidence, he wrote to thank his cousin Horace and gave a name to this ability to find things unexpectedly—serendipity.

The word *serendipity* is based on a fairy tale entitled *The Travels and Adventures of Three Princes of Serendip*. Serendip is an ancient name for the island nation Sri Lanka off India's southern coast. The king of the fable recognized that education requires more than learning from books, so he sent his sons out of the country to broaden their experience. Throughout the story, the clever princes carefully observed their surroundings and then used their knowledge in ways that saved them from danger and death.

For Walpole, serendipity meant finding, by chance, something valuable, using informed observation (sagacity). These are essentially "happy accidents." The word *serendipity* has many pop-culture references, most prominently the movie *Serendipity*, but many people don't know its original meaning or realize its usefulness. Walpole's ambiguous definition has invited a range of possible meanings, however.[14]

The study of serendipitous events requires a simplification of the exotic term. Serendipity is a coincidence form based upon action. It's not enough to imagine what you want or need. You have to move. A Spanish Gypsy proverb says it well: "The dog that trots about finds the bone." This capacity seems to sometimes rely on the human ability to find our way to places where there are people, ideas, or things that provide us with what we have been seeking. I call this our human geospatial positioning system (GPS) ability (more about this in chapter 8).

The four ingredients of serendipity are active searching (out of need or curiosity), chance, informed observation, and valued outcome. Dictionaries define chance as something fortuitous that happens unpredictably without discernible human intention. *La cheance,* in Old French, is derived from the Old Latin, *cadere,* meaning "to fall," implying that it is in the nature of things to fall, to settle out, or happen by themselves.[15] In her 2017 paper "On Serendipity in Science," Samantha Copeland of Delft University in the Netherlands defined chance as a deviation from expectation. She noted that serendipity in science and technology is often recognized retrospectively, only after the value of the observation is solidified.[16]

Serendipity, which is essentially one kind of meaningful coincidence (synchronicity being another), takes several forms. The primary form is accidentally finding something of interest or value. From this comes two major variations: (1) looking for something and finding it in an unexpected way and (2) looking for something and finding something entirely different. Sociologists Robert Merton and Elinor Barber wrote a delightful and scholarly history of the word *serendipity*. Their book is aptly titled *The Travels and Adventures of Serendipity,* which begins with Walpole and travels through bibliophiles, science, and the humanities.[17]

Copeland[18] suggested that these two variations share a fundamental characteristic: the intentions behind the activity taking place at the time of the unexpected observation or event are only indirectly related to the outcome.

An example of looking for something and finding it in an unexpected way is the famous case of penicillin. Microbiologist Alexander Fleming was actively searching for a new antibiotic in 1928. When he returned from vacation, he found penicillin juice killing bacteria in petri dishes that should have been washed while he was gone.[19] Walpole unexpectedly finding the Capello coat of arms is another example.

An example of looking for something and finding something else is the discovery of America. In 1492, Christopher Columbus sought a westward route to East Asia and found the New World instead. And Viagra was accidentally found while researchers in England in the 1990s were testing a new anti-hypertensive and anti-angina drug. Their male subjects reported increased and prolonged erections.[20] It became one of the best-selling drugs of all time.

Wilhelm Roentgen's discovery of X-ray is a perfect example of this type of serendipity. The German physicist was experimenting with cathode rays, which were popular in physics at the time. When he covered the cathode tube with black cardboard to hide its glow, he noticed a glimmer of light on a fluorescent screen across the room. Later, he replaced the screen with photographic paper and produced the first X-ray. "The genius of Roentgen consists in the fact that he immediately recognised an entirely new phenomenon," wrote V. Lakshminarayanan in the journal *Resonance*.[21] So the value of serendipity may be recognized immediately or in hindsight. The sagacity required for this discovery and many other serendipity-fueled findings is the investigator's ability to see the single instance as representing a universal pattern.

A variation involves noticing something in one situation and recognizing how that something can fill a need in another situation. In 1941 the Swiss electrical engineer George de Mestral wondered why Burdock seeds clung to his coat and dog; this wondering led to the invention of Velcro.

A long list of serendipities in science, technology, and the arts can be found in medical researcher Pek van Andel's paper in the *British Journal for the Philosophy of Science*.[22]

In the twentieth century, serendipity was involved in many major medical breakthroughs, according to Morton A. Meyers, M.D., emeritus professor of radiology and internal medicine at the State University of New York at Stony Brook, in his book *Happy Accidents*. Serendipity was involved with the discovery of X-rays, antidepressants, the pap smear, chemotherapy drugs, blood thinners, antibiotics, sterilized surgical fields, and much more. Regrettably the bureaucratization of research design through government grant applications stymies the blossoming of the accidental ways to discovery.[23]

In 2019, I attended the first meeting of the Serendipity Society in London. The society aims to establish a network of academics to promote and support rigorous research into all kinds of serendipity. Serendipity academics work in many different countries around the world. They can be found in psychology, psychiatry, library science, information science, physics, technology, business, economics, computer science, English, journalism, and science policy. People in the business and author communities are also involved. The society hopes to develop serendipity research as an independent field of study and be a resource of expertise on serendipity to which organizations, innovators, and planners can turn.[24]

Synchronicity and serendipity represent central aspects of meaningful coincidences but together do not encompass all of them. Both tend to focus on positive outcomes, but some coincidences offer no new information; others seem to promise something and don't deliver and some lead to destructive outcomes. (These problematic coincidences are discussed in chapter 9.) Other coincidences involve strings of observable objects that do not fit with either synchronicity or serendipity.

SERIALITY

The phenomenon of seriality differs from serendipity and synchronicity in that it is a series of events in the objective world that the mind takes note of and remembers. Unlike serendipity and synchronicity, there is not necessarily a special subjective element. The series of events could theoretically be verified by anyone.

Austrian biologist Paul Kammerer defined *seriality* as "a recurrence of the same or similar things or events in time and space" that "are not connected by the same acting cause." (This statement is a precursor of Jung's synchronicity principle.) However, Kammerer viewed these repetitions as simply natural phenomena. No one has described strings of similar events more thoroughly than Kammerer. He spent hours sitting on benches in various public parks, noting the people who passed by and classifying them by sex, age, dress, whether they carried umbrellas or parcels, and so on. He did the same during the long train rides from his home to his office in Vienna.

Kammerer was not particularly interested in meaning—only repeated sequences. His one hundred examples include apparently insignificant repetitions of numbers, names, words, and letters. Some examples:

His wife was in a waiting room reading about a painter named Schwalbach when a fellow patient named Mrs. Schwalbach was called into the consultation room.

His brother-in-law went to a concert and received cloakroom ticket number nine, which was the same number as his seat. Shortly thereafter he and his brother-in-law went to another concert and again his brother-in-law's cloakroom ticket number, twenty-one, matched his seat number.

On the train, Kammerer's wife was reading a novel with a character named "Mrs. Rohan." She saw a man get on the train who looked like their friend Prince Rohan. Later that night, the prince himself dropped by their house for a visit.[25]

Sometimes Kammerer described events that were clustered in space: Arthur Koestler recounted one such cluster in his book *The Case of the Midwife Toad*: "Case No. 10 concerns two young soldiers who had never met before. They were separately admitted to the military hospital of Ktowitze, Bohemia, in 1915. Both were nineteen, both had pneumonia, both were born in Silesia, both were volunteers in the Transport Corps, and both were called Franz Richter. Six items overlapped."[26]

In his 1919 book *Das Gesetz der Serie* (*The Law of Series*), Kammerer outlined these laws and provided a broad set of classifications of serial types and qualities. This work on seriality helped Jung develop his concept of synchronicity. Afterward Jung used a definition for synchronicity that was similar to Kammerer's definition of seriality. But Kammerer attributed the confluence of events to influences he thought were within the realm of known science,[27] while Jung relied on explanations outside known causal principles. Jung emphasized personal meaning, while Kammerer did not. Nevertheless, a series of improbable parallel events can seem quite meaningful. Meaningful series may take the form of a repeated phrase, seeing the same person in different contexts, or references to the same movie or book.

Seriality, synchronicity, and serendipity all rely on the recognition of similarity. Seriality applies to an observable sequence of similarities, like three people walking by with a yellow umbrella in a short period of time when it is not raining. These are public events. On the other hand, in synchronicity and serendipity, one of the two events is usually a private mental event, the other an observable public event.

SIMULPATHITY

The word *simulpathity* has a recent history. I coined the word to describe a personal experience that I soon realized many other people have experienced as well.

Late in the evening of February 26, 1973, when I was thirty-one years old, I found myself bent over the kitchen sink in an old Victorian house in San Francisco, choking on something that was caught in my throat. But there was nothing to cough up as I hadn't eaten anything. I choked for about fifteen minutes, a very long time, before I could swallow and breathe normally.

The next day, my birthday, my brother called to tell me that our father, three-thousand miles and three time zones away, had passed away in Wilmington, Delaware, just as I was choking in California. My father had bled into his throat and choked on his own blood. The timing led me to think that it couldn't possibility have been random.

Through reading and research, I could confirm that my experience with my father was no anomaly. The simultaneous experience by one person of the distress of another without conscious awareness and usually at a distance is not really uncommon. One person is in pain; the other begins to feel something similar without knowing why. Twins serve as a prototype for these kinds of experiences because the largest number of reports of this kind come from twins,[28] although there are similar stories about mothers and their children as well as other closely bonded pairs.[29]

The more than 2,500 respondents to the WCS that I constructed while at the University of Missouri reported that they "occasionally" experienced the pain of a loved one at a distance.[30] In Stevenson's review of 160 published simulpathity cases, one-third involved a parent and child. Friends and acquaintances were involved in about 28 percent. Husband and wife pairs were involved in about 14 percent and siblings about 15 percent. The similar relatively high percentages of parent-child and friend-acquaintance simulpathity suggests that emotional bonds, rather than genetic similarities, facilitate these interactions. Stevenson's reports are well-documented by follow-up interviews with both the coincider and the people who witnessed the event.[31]

I decided to name this coincidence pattern *simulpathity,* from the Latin word *simul,* which means "simultaneous," and the Greek root *pathy,* which means both "suffering" and "feeling," as in the words *sympathy* and *empathy.* With *sympathy* ("suffering together"), the sympathetic person is aware of the suffering of the other. With *simulpathity,* the person involved is usually not consciously aware of the suffering of the other (except for those pairs with whom this shared pain is a regular occurrence). Only later is the simultaneity of the distress recognized. No explanatory mechanism is implied. (The original meaning of *telepathy,* coined in 1882 by the classical scholar Fredric W. H. Myers, a founder of the Society for Psychical Research, was "distress communicated at a distance," as suggested by the suffix *pathy,* which also means "feeling, passion, affliction." But the definition has come to mean "thought transference."[32])

Jung was suddenly awoken by a dull headache "as though something had struck my forehead and then the back of my skull." The next day he received a telegram saying that his patient had shot himself in the head. The bullet had come to rest on the back wall of his skull.[33]

In one example, anthropological researchers Brett Mann and Chrystal Jaye reported in the journal *Anthropology and Medicine* that a study participant called Diana had become the protector and defender of her mildly intellectually handicapped twin brother through late primary school years. She somehow knew when he was in trouble and she knew to go help him. "At school I remember getting a bit sick of it and thinking, 'How can he look after himself instead of me having to look after him?'. . . And it's also a bit scary to have that kind of awareness . . . in terms of responsibility . . . I felt so responsible for him at an early age."[34]

Berthold E. Schwarz, an American neuropsychiatrist, documented many similar instances. In the 1960s he coined the term *telesomatic* to describe these events, from the Greek words meaning "distant body."[35] Similarly, individuals experience similar sensations or actual physical changes, even though they may be separated by great distances. The physician Larry Dossey suggests that a shared mind bridges the two bodies.[36]

How do we account for these simulpathity experiences? It appears that the two individuals involved are more closely bonded than current scientific thought holds people to be. Simulpathity reveals the existence of a kind of tunnel between minds. These incredible interpersonal connections point us toward a new view of reality.

3

Patterns of Coincidence

Humans seek coherent structure and order. We seek patterns by which to describe, predict, and control realities. Words and numbers order perceptions. Numbers on buildings define places on Earth. Numbers indicate values in athletics, academics, friendships, and business. Maps order space; clocks order time. Daily routines create predictable futures. The language of math can predict things, such as where two cars traveling toward each other on the same route will meet each other, given their speeds and starting locations. Words in sentences package complex experiences.

In a similar way, a taxonomy of coincidences organizes this complex territory into patterns from which order, usefulness, and explanation can emerge.

Coincidences are formed from two kinds of events: **mind** and **object**. **Mind** events are thoughts, feelings, emotions, sensations, and images. These are primarily private events. Mind includes emotions, like grief, and sensations, like pain, that can also be inferred from observations by others. **Object** events occur in the public sphere so that someone else could possibly observe them.

A **mind-object** coincidence is the most commonly reported form of coincidence. The coincider thinks, imagines, or feels something that is paralleled in an event outside their mind. To varying degrees each object has a form and a meaning that resonates with something in the mind of the coincider. They can be people, animals, plants, and inanimate objects like words in books, on the internet, and in speech and music. They can be lost or needed objects like keys and money. They can be visuals in real life, movies, plays, videos, photographs, paintings, and drawings. Objects can also be machines, divining cards, and in some cultures, animal entrails and tea leaves. Any observable event can become an object. The object has a shape similar to (is isomorphic with) something in the mind.

A **mind-mind** coincidence is one in which two people share the same thoughts, feelings, pains, or images. The coincidence is discovered when each relates the experience directly to the other or through an intermediary.

An **object-object** coincidence is one in which a series of two or more similar things, symbols, numbers, words, or combinations is perceived. Since objects are public, anyone, not just the coincider, can witness this coincidence form. Seriality is included with object-object coincidences.

Meta-coincidences are coincidences about coincidences.

What follows are anecdotes illustrating each of these coincidence categories. Some scholars will argue that a collection of anecdotes is just that, a series of anecdotes; some will (incorrectly) recall a famous quote that said, "The plural of anecdote is not data." Remarkably, the original quote from Stanford professor Raymond Wolfinger had the opposite meaning. In an email Wolfinger wrote, "I said, 'The plural of anecdote is data' sometime in the 1969–70 academic year while teaching a graduate seminar at Stanford. The occasion was a student's dismissal of a simple factual statement—by another student or me—as a mere anecdote. The quotation was my rejoinder."[1] So there you have it: the plural of anecdote *is* data.

A single incident, if true, usually represents a fact of human life.

Westerners, for example, once believed that all swans are white. Then, in 1697, the Dutch explorer Willem de Vlamingh discovered a black swan in Australia and that belief had to change. If one black swan existed, then there had to be others.[2] And, of course, there were.

The stories you are about to read harbinger the old idea about black swans, especially to people experiencing them for the first time. They seem odd, rare, unique, and hard to believe. Like black swans, if there is one, there is a high likelihood that there are others. Knowing that meaningful coincidences commonly occur will evaporate the fear of being negatively judged by others and free up coinciders to expect that listeners will respond with synchronicities and serendipities of their own.

MIND-OBJECT COINCIDENCES

An event in the mind is surprisingly correlated with an event in the surroundings. In these first anecdotes, *people are the object* of the coincidence.

Among the most delightful coincidences are those in which two strangers each need or desire an unknown somebody and that somebody serendipitously appears. Usually each person is actively seeking the desired other. Finding a love match in the swirls of human interaction may be the most celebrated of the mind-object type.

A close friend of mine was returning by plane to San Francisco after attending his father's tombstone unveiling on the East Coast. He was a few months away from finishing his psychiatric residency and had little idea about where to go and what to do after finishing. His future was wide open and blank. In those days, seats on airplanes were assigned, not personally selected. Seated in the same row was a young woman who asked him what time it was, even though she had a big watch on her wrist. She was returning from Chicago after an extended visit with her father. They found much in common. A few months later they moved together to Portland, Oregon, where she was going to graduate school. He simply wanted to go with her and have the freedom to paint. After a while, he found a psychiatric job there. They were married, had two children, and were together for forty years until they separated. At the time when they had met, each had in mind a readiness to find a permanent someone, and that person showed up. An image in each mind matched an object, a person, in the environment.

There are numerous other stories like this one. The settings for these dramas vary widely from a lonely beach, to a busy airport, to making the wrong turn and finding the right person. Sometimes it involves romance, other times work, and sometimes much needed help.

Author John Ironmonger told me this story: "I was researching for a new novel—a story that would touch on the collapse of civilization (later published as *Not Forgetting the Whale*) and I was reading a heavy book, *Collapse* by Jared Diamond. *Collapse* explores the reasons why ancient civilizations fell, often very suddenly, and I mined the book for helpful facts and observations. I decided to write to Jared Diamond (a Pulitzer Prize winner, by the way) to see if his research supported the central ideas of my story. But how should I contact him? I didn't have his email address, and who writes letters anymore? I knew he was a professor at UCLA so I tried a few variations of possible email addresses (you can guess the sort of thing— jared dot diamond at ucla dot org and so on). None of them worked. Oh well. The next week I set off on a vacation with my wife, Sue, and we traveled from England to Indonesia. In a small forest lodge in Sumatra, a long way from anywhere, we were almost the only guests. Almost. But not quite. Two keen bird-watchers were also there, and we shared a table for dinner. One of them (drumroll) turned out to be Jared Diamond! It was his seventy-fifth birthday. And he was very kind about my ideas."[3]

Animal as Object

In this next series of coincidences, *animals are the object*. For much of recorded human history animals have carried symbolic meanings. Sometimes mammals, birds, and insects seem to reflect human thought and emotion.

Birds may commemorate some human deaths. On June 12, 2016,

Omar Mateen, a twenty-nine-year-old security guard, killed forty-nine people and wounded fifty-three others in a mass shooting inside Pulse, a gay nightclub in Orlando, Florida. Orlando Police Department officers shot and killed him after a three-hour standoff. In a subsequent vigil, the names of the forty-nine victims were being read as a flock of birds flew by. A photographer noticed them and snapped a photo. Later, she counted the birds in the photo. There were forty-nine. The photographer showed other people and asked them to count. "We were all stunned," she said. A spokesman for the Dr. Phillips Center for the Performing Arts, where the vigil was held, said that the center had not released the birds during the vigil. The mind was the collective and individual grief of the mourners of forty-nine deaths. The object was the forty-nine birds.[4]

In his book *Synchronicity,* Jung described three instances of birds visiting the houses of three relatives of the same woman at the time of each of their deaths. These stories were told to him by the wife of one of his patients. At the time of death of both the woman's grandmother and mother, a number of birds gathered outside their death chambers. In describing these bird visitations at the times of these deaths, the woman became concerned about the health of her husband and encouraged him to seek a medical consultation. No medical problem was discovered, and yet on his way home from the appointment, his wife noticed that a flock of birds had alighted on their house. The birds triggered in her fears for her husband's life. And at at that moment, the man collapsed and died. Birds had once again accompanied the death of one of her relatives.[5]

Insects, too, can show up as they are being thought about. Mythologist Joseph Campbell lived in Greenwich Village in Manhattan on the fourteenth floor of a high-rise building. His study had two sets of windows, one of which overlooked the Hudson River. The other two windows faced Sixth Avenue and were hardly ever opened. One day Joseph was working on a chapter on the mythology of the African Bushmen of the Kalahari Desert. In that mythology, the praying mantis is a central, heroic figure. He was surrounded by articles about and pictures of the praying mantis. As he was working on this, he suddenly had an impulse to open one of the windows on the side that he never opened. He looked out of the window, turned his head to the right without really knowing why, and there on the wall of the fourteenth floor of the high-rise building was a praying mantis. Joseph said the praying mantis seemed to give him a meaningful look, and then continued up the wall. The element of the mind in this story was Joseph's intense concentration on the idea of the praying mantis; the object was a praying mantis on the wall.[6]

Inanimate Things as Object

Sometimes *inanimate things* are the object. Minds hold images of needed and lost things. Needed money and lost things somehow appear.

Nathan Stein had wanted to be a doctor but the Great Depression forced him to give up his dream. He pinned his hopes on his grandson Kevin who decided at a very early age to go to medical school. But Nathan died when Kevin was nine. As a senior at Penn State University, Kevin was confronted with enormous tuition costs. His parents, both real estate agents, stepped up their efforts to bring in more business. One day his father, Sherman, noticed an ad by people planning to sell their house on their own. Although he rarely contacted private sellers, he felt an uncontrollable urge to make an appointment with them.

After two appointment changes, Sherman met with the seller. With the address in hand, he had a strange feeling. As he walked up to the front door, he realized that this was his father-in-law's old house! As Sherman was telling the sellers about this coincidence, the doorbell rang. It was the mailman with a registered letter for Nathan Stein who had died fourteen years earlier. Sherman signed for it. The letter was from a bank about Nathan Stein's dormant account. The account contained the exact amount Kevin needed to go to medical school. In this story, the mind included the intentions of four people—the pre-med student, his parents, and his deceased grandfather. The object was the right amount of money to be able to attend medical school.[7]

Physical Place as Object

Physical places are sometimes the object of a coincidence. Real estate in the form of houses, apartments, and offices serendipitously meet the eyes of the hunter.

A sales representative for a drug company told me about her home-finding adventure: "My husband and I decided to buy and fix up the house we were currently renting. It was an okay place and seemed like the easiest thing to do. We drove to the bank and started the process of taking out a loan. On our way back to the house, my husband decided to go a different, longer way back. He said later he just felt like taking the alternate route. I spotted a woman putting up a 'For Sale' sign for her house right as we passed by. We stopped. It was just what I wanted. We bought it! It was just the right place for our family."

Media as Object

Various *media* can be the object of a coincidence. Media create many possible matches between mind and object. Among the four most frequent items on the WCS were: "I think of a question only to have it answered by an external source (i.e., radio, TV, or other people) before I can ask it" and "I think of an idea and hear or see it on the radio, TV, or internet."[8]

Actress Sissy Spacek never liked being told what to do. So when singer Loretta Lynn started telling gossip columnists and hosts of day-time and nighttime talk shows that Sissy was going to play Loretta in the movie *A Coal Miner's Daughter*, even though no such deal had been made, Sissy made sure to meet this woman. They met for the first time in a parking lot outside Loretta's tour bus in Shreveport, Louisiana. The power of Loretta's personality instantly convinced Sissy to play this woman! But she had misgivings too. How could she play a real person who was still living? The director then told her she didn't fit the part, but Universal Studios was still pressing her to take the part, as was her agent. Her manager was advising against it.

In the middle of this tense push and pull, Sissy and her husband, Jack, flew to Washington, D.C., to visit his mom, Gerri. She lived in a high-rise apartment building and drove a big white Cadillac and didn't like country music. Her car radio was always tuned to classical. She knew little about Loretta. When she heard Sissy's dilemma, she suggested prayer. Sissy jokingly asked for a sign from God.

Watching television later that evening, they saw Loretta tell late-night talk show host Johnny Carson that Sissy would take the role. Exasperated, Sissy asked Jack to go for a drive with her. As they drove away in Gerri's Cadillac, the radio started up with Loretta singing "A Coal Miner's Daughter." Somehow Gerri's classical music station had turned into something else. Sissy decided then and there to do the movie, and in 1980 she won the Oscar for Best Actress in that movie.[9] Mind was trying to resolve the conflict and object was the song on the radio.

Machine as Object

Sometimes *machines* are the object in a mind-object coincidence. Machines seem to respond to human emotions. At 10:10 a.m. on June 25, 2010, in the Oval Office, President Obama heard the news that the Supreme Court had supported the continuation of the Affordable Care Act. It was the signature act of his presidency. He and his staff celebrated. At 10:30 a.m., photographs by the official staff photographer showed that the clock in the office had stopped at 10:10 a.m.[10]

Disease as Object

A *disease* can be the object of a coincidence. Successful medical researchers focus on a specific idea, elevating desire for knowledge of it to the forefront of their thinking. Some researchers take up a project because it is personally relevant.

Having practiced medicine as a professor of clinical medicine at the University of California–San Francisco early in her career, Elisabeth Targ's studies drew her to probe the possible role of the mind-body-spirit connection involved in medical healing. No project captured her enthusiasm and commitment more than her study of the possible efficacy of prayer in healing. Through randomized double-blind clinical trials, she and her colleagues found strong evidence that AIDS patients, who received prayers from distant healers of a variety of faiths, had significantly better medical outcomes than patients who did not receive supportive prayers.

Then, in 1997, Targ designed a study and secured funding from the National Institutes of Health (NIH) to explore distant healing and prayer as trainable skills that nurses and other health professionals might integrate into their healing work. Principally, the study examined the efficacy of prayer on patients with a rare and difficult-to-treat form of brain cancer, glioblastoma. Shortly after receiving funding from the NIH, Targ herself was diagnosed with this same form of cancer. But healing prayer, radiation, and chemotherapy were not able to stop this rapidly growing cancer. She died shortly before her forty-first birthday.[11]

Mind was Elisabeth's strong mental focus on glioblastoma healing and the object was her own glioblastoma.

Future Event as Object

A *future event* is the object in some coincidences. Some people seem to be able to anticipate future events in yet-to-be-explained ways. These precognitions may be best considered probability estimates of a possible occurrence, not certainties. People tend to remember the hits and forget the misses. The time spans for predicting events in the future vary from seconds to years.

Brian Inglis gathered coincidence stories for his book titled *Coincidence* primarily from reports to the Koestler Foundation. He found this one about a split-second lifesaving move: As a war correspondent in the Nigerian civil war, thriller novelist Frederick Forsythe had the uncomfortable feeling that he was being stared at. He could not see anyone. Suddenly he heard a timber post twenty yards away topple over. He jerked his head to the left to see what happened. At that moment he felt a bullet whiz by and thump into the door jam. Had he not moved his head to the left, the bullet would have entered his skull. He checked out the post. It had been destroyed by termites. "One termite must have given the last nibble that separated the last strand of wood," said Forsythe.[12] Mind was the desire to not be injured. Object was the sound that made Forsythe move.

A retired seaman, named Morgan Robertson, published a book in 1898 entitled *The Wreck of the Titan: Or, Futility*. His novel described the maiden voyage of a transatlantic luxury liner named *Titan*. Although it was touted as being unsinkable, the ship struck an iceberg and sank with much loss of life. In 1912, the *Titanic,* a transatlantic luxury liner widely touted as unsinkable, struck an iceberg on her maiden voyage and sunk with great loss of life. In Robertson's book, the disaster took place in April, just as it did in the real event. In the book there were 3,000 passengers aboard the ship; on the *Titanic,* 2,207.[13] In the book, there were 24 lifeboats; on the *Titanic,* 20. Robertson must have been familiar with the possibility that ships this size could be built. But the name of the ship and the iceberg were much harder to know.

Mind was Robertson's imagining the story of *Titan*. Object was the real-life story of the *Titanic*. The coincidence goes further than that, too: many people scheduled for the 1912 inaugural sailing of the doomed ship the *Titanic* had premonitions of disaster. Mind was image of disaster and object was the sinking of the Titanic.[14]

MIND-MIND COINCIDENCES

Mind-mind coincidences include shared thoughts, shared emotions and physical sensations, and human GPS, the name I give to the ability to get where one needs to be at the right time without consciously planning to get there.

Twins, especially identical twins, report the highest frequency of mind-mind coincidences. They share strong psychological as well as strong physical simultaneous parallels at a distance. Their minds and bodies seem to be linked; it's as if they are each part of the same body. They shared, after all, almost exactly the same primary life experience together—growing in their mother's uterus at the same time and entering the outside world around the same time.[15]

The British writer Guy Lyon Playfair has summarized the research conducted on twin telepathy. In 2004, a survey by the department of twin research and genetic epidemiology of King's College, London (DTR) elicited more than five thousand replies. The twins were asked "if they had the ability to know what was happening to their partner." Nearly 40 percent of the twins replied yes, and a further 15 percent were "convinced" of it.

Playfair summarized the research of Mary Rosambeau who, in preparation of her book *How Twins Grow Up,* created a lengthy newspaper appeal for answers to her twin questionnaire. She received six hundred replies. Her questionnaire on many aspects of twin activity included these two questions:

1. Have you or your twin(s) had any experience which might be explained as being able to read each other's minds? If so, what?
2. Have you ever been surprised by both of you having the same illness or pain at the same time?

The 183 "yes" replies included these categories:

1. "Knowing" when one twin is about to telephone the other.
2. Saying the same thing at the same time; singing a song the other was just thinking of.
3. Using identical words when replying to the same exam question after doing the same homework.
4. They "just knew" that their other was in trouble. They commented, "I felt something was wrong," "I felt very uneasy," or "I was overcome with misery."
5. They seem to share the same dream.
6. They share the same pain or injury.

More detailed subsequent surveys with twins from DTR gave clear support to these findings. While a surprising number of fraternal, or dizygotic (two fertilized eggs) twins reported instances of both telepathy and shared dreams, monozygotic (both growing from one fertilized egg) twins reported almost twice as many of each.[16]

A remarkable story was related by Playfair in which a six-year-old girl with a plainly visible black eye was assuring her mother that she had not had an accident and felt no pain. Around the same time her twin sister had been involved in a playground tumble that had left her with an even blacker eye (the same one) and considerable pain. This was filmed at the time and later shown on television.[17] The body image in the mind of the injured twin was so strongly implanted in her sister's mind that it seemed to cause a similar body image in her mind and a similar looking injury.

A horrible version of shared emotion and behavior involves twins Remus and Romulus. Remus became so angry at his wife that he tried to strangle her but ended up stabbing her to death. At almost the same time his brother Romulus was out with his girlfriend with whom he apparently had a calmer relationship. Romulus suddenly felt compelled by some unknown force to strangle her to death.[18] The impulse in the mind of Remus seemed to have stirred up a similar impulse in the mind of Romulus.

Shared events like these occur in the general (non-twin) population as well; as mentioned in the simulpathity description, they are probably related to the degree of bonding between the two people at the time of the event. A thought, emotion, or body injury can be mirrored in another person at a distance around the same time. These are obviously mind-mind coincidences.

For example, many people find that they start thinking about a particular person for no apparent reason, then the phone rings and that person is on the line. Or else when the telephone starts ringing, they have an intuition about who is calling, and it turns out to be correct.[19]

Biologist Rupert Sheldrake formalized this kind of research. He and Pamela Smart recruited people willing to guess which one of four selected callers was the current caller. The experimental subjects selected at least two known people to be part of the group of four. A die was rolled to select one of the four. They made 231 correct guesses in 571 trials, a success rate of 40 percent, well above the mean chance expectation of 25 percent. Greater emotional closeness predicted greater ability to correctly guess which one of four possible people was calling.[20]

Simultaneous Activities

Two emotionally connected people *doing the same thing at the same time at a distance* is clearly a coincidence. SQuire Rushnell tells the story of Christopher and Marion, who were still reeling from divorces each had gone through around the same time. They felt good with each other but the fear of intimacy kept them wavering. And they lived two thousand miles apart. Yet they knew that marriage looked like an increasingly likely possibility. One day, Christopher stood trance-like in front of his bookshelf. He picked up *The Nature of Love* and randomly turned to a page discussing the writings of Kahlil Gibran. He read, "Give your hearts, but not into each other's keeping, for only the hand of Life can contain your hearts." He called Marion and read the lines to her. She paused and told him: "I am, right now, holding the same book in my lap . . . *The Nature of Love* . . . and the only part of the book I have read is the part you have just read to me."[21] His mind was on the same idea as her mind.

Simulpathity

Simulpathity experiences are prototypical mind-mind coincidences. Strong emotions and physical injuries seem to press the telepathy "send" button.

This first story comes from Brian Inglis's book *Coincidence: A Matter of Chance—Or Synchronicity?* Having dinner with a friend, "Joan Harper" recalls that she was expecting to stay until 11 in the evening before going back home to her husband. "I was just about to begin eating when I had the strongest feeling I should return home immediately." She decided not to ignore this feeling, and arrived home to find her husband in the midst of a medical emergency.

Because she returned home, she was able to get medical help and he survived.[22] The terror in her husband's mind had registered in Joan Harper's mind.

Jungian therapist Rob Hopcke tells of a patient named Jerry, with whom therapy had ended a year previously. Then Hopcke dreamed of Jerry lying in bed in a beach house, breathing slowly. A short time after Hopcke had the dream, Jerry decided to return to therapy and told Hopcke of his suicide attempt at a hotel near the ocean. He had lain in bed in the ocean-side hotel for three days before waking up. Hopcke consulted his dream diary, which confirmed that Jerry had made the suicide attempt the same week that Hopcke had dreamed of Jerry being in a beach house.[23] The images in Jerry's mind of his emotional reality appeared in Hopcke's dreaming mind.

Jung reported a similar event. One of his acquaintances dreamed of the sudden death of one of his friends. The death was confirmed the next day by telegram.[24]

The intense emotions of death seem to further increase the potential for information to be received by a bonded other person. In the 1930s Rose Rudkin, living in London, woke up knowing her mother, living in Ohio, had died. Rose did not know how she knew. A cablegram soon arrived confirming this impression. Psychiatrist Ian Stevenson corroborated most of this story through correspondences with Mrs. Rudkin and her son as well as the mother's death certificate.[25] The feeling of dying in her mother's mind appeared in her daughter's mind.

Thoughts

A *thought* can be mirrored in another mind in the same place. Telepathy usually refers to mental events at a distance. It also happens in numerous situations including psychotherapy, in the classroom, and with animals. Since telepathy is not recognized by mainstream science, telepathic events, which clearly do happen, are regarded as just a coincidence. But once science recognizes telepathy and other psi events as real, these events will no longer be regarded as mere coincidences.

Sigmund Freud considered thought-transference, or telepathy, to have a "kernel of truth." "One is led to the suspicion that this [telepathy] is the original archaic method of communication between individuals and that in the course of phylogenetic evolution it has been replaced by the better method of giving information with the help of signals which are picked up by the sense organs. But the older method might have persisted in the background."[26] He had years earlier criticized Jung for his interest in the paranormal. The subject continues to be considered worthy of study within psychoanalysis.[27]

In addition to psychotherapy, other situations also hold the potential for telepathy. One of them is the classroom. Marcus Anthony, Ph.D., is an author and a practicing spiritual counselor. He teaches in China, Hong Kong, and other East Asian locations. He told me this story during our radio interview. Anthony assigned his class of fourteen-year-old boys to write the first line of a mystery story. That night Anthony had a dream that "the police were on the lookout for Jack the Ripper." The mood of the dream was dark and somber. He awoke with the feeling of it fresh in his mind.

On the road to school, his car pulled behind another vehicle with a sticker on the back that read "Jack is back." It was an ad for whisky.

In class, he looked around to sense where the "energy" was. His intuition confidently designated James as the place to start. "James began to tell the story of a woman who had been brutally murdered. 'The police went on a hunt for the man responsible. They found him and tried to arrest him, but he fought back. The policeman fired, and the man fell to the ground screaming. As he fell silent and death overtook him, a dark and horrible shadow rose out of the dead man's body. It was the spirit of Jack the Ripper!'"

Marcus commented: "That synchronicity invited me to face the part of me that had been deeply hurt by certain female figures from my childhood. I came to see that at a very profound level I had been psychically emasculated by the women who had raised me, and that the experience had left me with a deep-seated lust for revenge that I had not been fully acknowledging. The anger was then preventing me from forming intimate relationships with women in my adulthood."[28]

Many dog owners think that their dogs can read their minds.[29] Perhaps we can also read their minds. As I was leaving the house of a friend of mine who was getting married a few weeks later, I looked at his dog, a female Rhodesian Ridgeback, who was looking directly at me. Spontaneously and without thinking, I asked her out loud, "Are you going to be the flower bearer?" Surprised, my friend, the dog's owner, said "Yes!" I was surprised too. Perhaps she had an image in her mind that I could pick up with my mind.

Rosalyn W. Berne is an associate professor in the department of engineering and society's program of science, technology, and society (STS) at the University of Virginia. She is also an equine empath. This new identity began after she fell off a horse while they were crossing a river in Costa Rica. The horse appeared to be concerned, and she thought she heard the question: "Are you alright?" Was she hearing things? Then she heard the horse say that this never happens to him. He continued: "Now I am being taken off the riding circuit for more training. I just need a rest." Rosalyn told the owner who was very surprised. How did Rosalyn know the horse was to be taken away for more training? The horse had told her. After many tests of her communication ability between horse and human, Rosalyn came to have conversations with numerous horses. She has helped many owners develop loving relationships with these highly intelligent creatures. Her mind is able to connect with the minds of horses.[30]

Subconscious Physical Mirroring

Subconscious physical mirroring is when people experience similar bodily pains while in the same place. This experience is more than empathy. Their bodies seem to be experiencing the same thing at the same time.

Couvade is the name given to the experiencing by men of the sicknesses associated with their partner's pregnancy. In a study by researchers at Memorial University in Canada, women who were expecting a baby and their male partners were found to have similar levels of the hormones prolactin and cortisol in the period just before their baby was born. After the births, the mothers and fathers had lower concentrations of sex steroids (testosterone and estradiol). Men with sympathetic pregnancy symptoms had higher prolactin levels and greater reductions in testosterone.[31]

Here is a story of a woman who had tried for five years to become pregnant. One day her husband woke up feeling nauseous at the smell of breakfast. He rushed to the bathroom to vomit. He repeated the scene the next morning. Did he have an ulcer? No. But she was pregnant. He was experiencing morning sickness and she was not. His symptoms continued for the next four months, while she had none. His symptoms persisted even when he was miles away from her.[32] He felt the symptoms in his own mind and body that were normally experienced by the pregnant woman.

Twins may also experience couvade when one of them is pregnant.[33] Call it physiological empathy or local simulpathity.

OBJECT-OBJECT COINCIDENCES

The mind-object and mind-mind categories involve at least one private event, observable only by the coincider. Each element of an object-object coincidence is potentially observable by a third person. The primary objects include both living beings and inanimate things.

Hiring new people can be a chancy adventure. As head of psychiatry at the University of Missouri, I had to find and hire new faculty members. The usual process involved advertising in psychiatric newspapers and making phone calls to colleagues in other cities. My method was different. Most of the faculty I hired had contacted our department to see if there was a job open in our department. I liked relying on the coincidental timing of our department's need and the prospecting psychiatrist's desire to work with us. I hired each of the five women who contacted us. Their collective stories were particularly striking. Soon after accepting the position, each of the five became pregnant. The second, third, and fourth each had twins. The fifth had been trying to get pregnant for several years. She, too, became pregnant soon after being hired, but unlike most of the others, she had a single child.

There is one possible explanation for this: when women of childbearing age find satisfying work, they become more relaxed and more able to conceive children, so having a new job can increase the likelihood of becoming pregnant. But the string of twins that occurred here becomes more surprising, however. To follow a basketball analogy: in a single game when a player reaches double digits in points, assists, and rebounds, it is called a triple-double. My department scored a triple-double—three women with twins.

The first woman, who had a single baby, stayed for a few years then took a job that paid twice as much in a warmer climate. Her departure represented a major loss to the department. The fifth woman joyfully raised her single child but stayed with us for less than two years because her husband found a better job elsewhere. The families of the triple-double stayed. The three women went on to make outstanding contributions to the department. Three women who had gotten a new job in our department each had the same experience: pregnancy with twins and longevity as faculty members.

In another example, a patient of mine was struggling with alcoholism. As with any pattern in need of deliberate change, the person must recognize the pattern and decide to change. She was reluctant to consider doing anything about it and stopped coming in to see me. She sank more deeply into self-pity. Then, over the course of a few days, she found herself being inundated with images about drinking problems. She saw an old movie, *The Days of Wine and Roses*, which showed the steady decline of a woman from loving chocolate to becoming addicted to alcohol. She was told about a distant relative who recently died of complications from excessive alcohol. She barely avoided being hit by a beer delivery truck. She cut her foot on a broken whiskey bottle. As she sat in a coffee shop, she overheard a conversation about Alcoholics Anonymous (AA). After witnessing this string of events, she took the hint and started going to AA meetings. Knowing my interest in coincidences and in her, she let me know what happened. These objects were all public events.

Ideas

Simultaneous independent inventions and discoveries tell us that if one person has thought of a new idea, the likelihood is high that someone else has thought of it or will soon think of it. One simple explanation: the problems of the age attract problem solvers of the age, all of whom work within the same constraints and use the currently available theories and technologies to solve the problems. Additionally, human minds are connected and subconsciously communicate through a collective consciousness (see chapter 12 for more on this topic).

Many instances throughout history illustrate this coincidence type. Calculus was independently formulated by Newton, Leibniz, and others around the same time in the seventeenth century. Oxygen was discovered by Scheele, Priestley, Lavoisier, and others at the same time in the eighteenth century. Darwin and Wallace both proposed the theory of evolution at the same time in the nineteenth century. On February 14, 1876, Elisha Gray and Alexander Graham Bell independently, the same day, filed patents for the invention of the telephone. These examples and many others were catalogued in 1922![34] There have been so many more examples since then. In the end, the first person to publicize the discovery or invention usually gets the credit.

In March of 1951, cartoonists in the United States and England introduced audiences to a trouble-causing little boy named Dennis, each of whom had a dog who helped create the chaos. Both called the comic strip "Dennis the Menace." An article on the website Plagiarism Today states: "Though . . . many draw the conclusion that one of the two creators had to have plagiarized the other, it's become clear that simply wasn't the case. Not only did the two creators have no way of knowing what the other was working on, but the two characters are actually extremely different." That's true in terms of their attitudes, though not their results. The British Dennis intentionally caused trouble, while the American Dennis, always good-natured and angelic, consistently stumbled into trouble. Both boys were immensely popular. They each had hit a cultural pleasure nerve—the archetypal bad boy.[35]

The objects in each example are ideas that were independently discovered or invented.

Numbers

Gary Schwartz, a psychology professor at the University of Arizona, finds long strings of object-object coincidences. He wisely suggests that he may be holding certain objects in the forefront of his mind that make him more ready to find them. In his book *Super Synchronicity,* he described sequences of more than six *objects* involving the number eleven: dragonflies, bears, ducks, ravens, and the word *synchronicity.*[36]

Are numbers inherent properties of reality or marks human minds have put on reality? No one knows. For some people number coincidences are packed with metaphysical meaning.[37] For most people, they are common occurrences in everyday reality. We are literally surrounded by numbers. Time, weather, radio and TV stations, street numbers, home and work addresses, telephone numbers, bills, rent, mortgage payments, groceries and other household purchases, birthdays, anniversaries, deaths, book pages, bank accounts, savings, credit and debit cards, passwords, debt, financial losses, and others. With so many sources of numbers, strings of specific ones are likely. Whether they are noticed or not varies.

Some number strings, especially those within a certain category like time or money, seem more likely to capture people's attention and imagination. People report that they regularly notice certain numbers on their clocks like 11:11, 2:22, 3:33, 4:44, 5:55, 2:30, and 9:11. Their awareness of the number seems to create their being alert to finding the same number again. Each number recurs twice on a twelve-hour clock, so there are repeated opportunities to notice any one of them.

While I was writing this section on numbers, in fact, my son Karlen called to tell me about my grand dog Walter's current medical condition. We hung up and my phone said 11:11. Later that day, I opened my phone to electronically send payment to him for the veterinarian. The time was 1:11. The objects were 11:11 and 1:11.

Names

Like numbers, names can repeat themselves, sometimes in long strings of five or more. In his book *When God Winks on Love,* SQuire Rushnell tells Jerry's story about the name Kimberly. His wife Kimberly had asked for a divorce. He reluctantly signed the divorce papers. After a few years he started dating another Kimberly. The relationship drifted. He decided to drive three hours to his sister's house, also named Kimberly. Before leaving, he stopped at the cleaners. His ex-wife Kimberly was just leaving. Then, before he got back into his truck to leave town, his former girl-friend Kimberly was nearby and came to chat. He stopped at Kmart to get some film. Behind him in line was another woman named Kimberly. He then got some gas. He went to pay. The cashier was named Kimberly. Five Kimberlys within an hour. And then his future wife came into his life. Her name is Kimberly.[38] The objects were the name Kimberly.

Animals

A Baltimore-area author and manuscript editor contacted me about her coincidences. We met several times and kept in email contact. She told me the following story about a series involving monkeys, her totem animal. "My remarkable string of coincidences began in 2010 after I said a strikingly simple but deeply soulful prayer asking for guidance. That afternoon, and every day since, I've seen what could be described as a 'totem animal' which serves as a marker along my life's path. These are not nebulous visions or voices but instead tangible and traceable references—in books, on blogs, on billboards, in song lyrics, in television dialogue, and in the manuscripts I edit. These blocks of text unfold daily (up to ten times per day!), lovingly providing guideposts as I navigate my personal life, while also gifting me with lessons in divine spiritual law. They communicate with me predominantly through metaphor but with clarity and intelligence. Some of the messages are served up with brevity in snappy slogans and such, and yet others are profoundly allegorical and archetypal. I continue to document them in what is now a collection of many journals. This phenomenal series of synchronicities has cracked my psyche wide open and taken me on an extreme journey of awakening to universal truths."[39]

Plants

Some plants produce psychoactive chemicals that act similarly to the chemicals in human brains. Opiates, originally derived from the opium poppy, have been used for thousands of years for both recreational and medicinal purposes. The most active substance in opium is morphine—named after Morpheus, the Greek god of dreams. Codeine is the second most active. They stimulate opiate receptors in the brain to create pain relief, good feeling, and addiction.

Endorphins produced by the brains of humans and other vertebrates are responsible for the good feeling many people experience after a hard workout. The word *endorphin* comes from putting together the words *endogenous,* meaning "from within the body," and *morphine.* In other words, endorphins got their name because they stimulate the same receptors in the human brain that opium stimulates.[40]

The same is true with marijuana. Humans and animals alike naturally synthesize endocannabinoids, chemical compounds that activate the same receptors as delta-9-tetrahydrocannabinol (THC), one of the psychoactive components of marijuana.[41]

The two objects are exogenous and endogenous chemicals that stimulate the same brain receptors. Manufacturing chemicals that resonate with human brain receptors may have been an adaptation that assured the cultivation of the plants making the chemical. Still the question remains: How did the opium and cannabis plants come to making their substances in the first place?

Full Circle

Sometimes the spirals of life events, spinning through time, link past and present in surprising ways. In *Beyond Coincidence: Amazing Stories of Coincidence and the Mystery and Mathematics Behind Them,* Martin Plimmer and Brian King recount the story of Allan Cheek, an employee eager to advance, who had to choose between right and wrong. After Cheek's first promotion, his boss congratulated him on his successes and described the next project—to deceive a prospective investor out of a substantial amount of money. Cheek refused, threatening to resign if his boss went ahead with the scheme. The boss insisted. Despite his need for the job, Cheek resigned and then drove 180 miles to warn the unsuspecting victim. The potential victim had trouble believing the accusations. Cheek left, saying that he had done all he could do.

Two years later, Cheek was working for another company that entered into hard times. Money had been foolishly spent and a large debt incurred. The chairman of the board was about to close down the company. Cheek saw a way out, wrote a report describing how the company could prosper, and discussed it with the chairman. After several hours of intense negotiation, the chairman fired the CEO and put Cheek in charge.

With very little cash at his disposal, Cheek's first step was to move out of their expensive offices to less costly ones. He found an advertisement for three small offices over a garage and went to look at them. They were barely adequate, and even at the much lower cost, the company couldn't afford them. He asked the landlord to share his faith in the nearly bankrupt company by allowing him to defer payment.

"What did you say your name was?" asked the landlord.

"Allan Cheek."

"Two years ago, did you warn a man that he was about to be swindled?"

"Yes."

"That was my brother. He would've lost his life savings. Move in when you like and pay me when you can."

Four years later, the company had paid the landlord, paid off its debt, and moved to bigger offices.[42]

The integrative medicine physician Andrew Weil told me this story. As a young physician he was exploring the jungles of South America, looking at the healing methods of local shamen. He decided to take a few days rest in a hotel in Colombia, South America, that was run by two German women. The sisters presented him with an utterly delicious cheesecake. After he left, he had wished he had asked them for the recipe, but he did not know their names, so could not contact them.

Decades later, he was conducting a seminar in Philadelphia, Pennsylvania. A young physician began to speak with him. She was from Colombia. He asked where in Colombia she had come from. A few more questions and he discovered that the two women he had met long ago were this woman's great-grandmother and her great-grandaunt. And she had the cheesecake recipe!

Doppelgangers

Doppelgangers ("double goers" in German) are two strangers who share a remarkable number of characteristics; most commonly they look like identical twins. Fiction contains characters who are eerie mirror images of each other, like *Tale of Two Cities* by Charles Dickens.[43]

One of Kammerer's examples of seriality (described in chapter 2), which describes two soldiers who shared the same age, city of origin, job description, illness, first name, last name, and physical resemblance, also illustrates the doppelganger. If you want to find someone who looks like you, there are facial recognition websites that promise to connect you with someone who looks like you. Many others promise to find a celebrity look-a-like for you. However successful these search engines might be, in a population of seven billion there has to be some stranger who strongly resembles you out there somewhere. Your doppelganger may not yet be in the databases, but there has to be at least one twin for most of us. Perhaps someone will research this question.

META-COINCIDENCES

Coincidences can be about coincidences; these are meta-coincidences. The *meta* prefix is meant to indicate that one coincidence is somehow commenting on or connecting with the other one. The simpler of the two forms involves a coincidence experienced by a person in the course of studying coincidences. The more complicated meta-coincidences involve a pair of coincidences, usually occurring within a short time window, in which the content of one coincidence is directly related to the content of the other. The content does not necessarily involve the idea of coincidence.

Coincidences about the Subject of Coincidences

Here it is in its simplest form. One time, an email correspondent wrote to me: "There are coincidences everywhere," just as I was editing a paragraph with those very words. It's the timing that stood out on this coincidence.

In another version of the same pattern, an organizational consultant with whom I was once again corresponding received an email from Academia.edu, an online for-profit organization that connects academics through mutual interest. The email contained one of my coincidence research papers defining the characteristics of coincidence-sensitive people. This person is highly sensitive to coincidences. He and I had not been corresponding for several years.

On June 19, 2016, I met with a man who was advising me about the social group to whom I would present a synchronicity talk. He told me that day, June 19, was his son's twenty-ninth birthday. I told him that day was also my son's twenty-ninth birthday. An object-object coincidence. One object was meeting on June 19. The other object was both sons were born on June 19, 1986.

My book proposal for *Connecting with Coincidence* was rejected by Simon and Schuster. The editors said it was too much like their Eben Alexander's book *Proof of Heaven*. Since his was about his near-death experience and mine was about coincidences, I could not see the overlap. Two days later I received a text message from an ex-patient who had not contacted me for about eighteen months. "I am stuck in an airport for 8 hours so I picked up a book called *Proof of Heaven* which reminded me of your work with coincidences." So I asked him what the similarity was. He replied, "You both are physicians pointing out the limits of current scientific thought. You are each trying to say that there is something more to consciousness than we currently realize. You are running up against entrenched interests." My question was answered in this comment about my book, a meta-coincidence.

When One Coincidence Comments on Another

Sometimes a meta-coincidence involves *two coincidences that are directly related to one another*. George D. Bryson checked into a hotel in Louisville, Kentucky, having never been there and wanting to look around. He was taking the train from St. Louis to New York City. He was advised to go to the Brown Hotel. He was assigned room 307. "Just for fun" he asked for his mail. He was handed a letter addressed to "Mr. George D. Bryson, Room 307." It turned out, the previous day, another George D. Bryson had checked out of Room 307.[44]

The first coincidence was object-object. One object was the same name and the other object was the same room. The second coincidence was mind-object. Mind was Bryson's intuition to ask for his mail. The object was the letter for the other George Bryson. The same name coincidence that was revealed by asking for the letter informed him of the name–room number coincidence.

In another example, I was talking with a new acquaintance and manager at a local natural foods store, named Bill, on February 14, Valentine's Day. We discovered that each of us was interested in coincidences. He told me a coincidence involving a woman who earlier that day was looking for the complete quote of a saying from the poet Rumi. She had then gone to yoga class shortly afterward and heard her yoga teacher complete the quote.

At dance class the next day, I asked a new friend, Elle, how her Valentine's Day had gone. She told me about needing to find the full quote of a saying, and before she could say anything else, I said, "And your yoga teacher supplied it." Naturally, she was surprised, as was I, since neither of us knew that she and the manager of the store knew each other.

The line she knew was: *"Out beyond ideas of wrongdoing and rightdoing."*

What the yoga teacher supplied was: *"there is a field. I'll meet you there."*[45]

Two days later, I was to be interviewed by a filmmaker about coincidences. So I asked Elle if she would be willing to join me in the film. She accepted. On camera we talked about the Rumi coincidence and ended the interview by dancing together.

Talking with Bill let me know about the coincidence involving an unnamed woman and her yoga teacher. This information allowed me to create the coincidence with Elle by completing her sentence about the yoga teacher who coincidentally supplied the desired line from the poem. The coincidence between Elle and me, then, became a comment on the Elle–yoga teacher coincidence creating a meta-coincidence.

Again, these broad coincidence categories—object-mind, mind-mind, object-object, and meta-coincidences—are intended to help you recognize that your strange coincidence is an example of a particular kind of coincidence as well as a springboard for future investigations.

4

Coincidence Sensitivity

Not everyone is aware of coincidences. So the question arises: What circumstances and personality traits make coincidences likely to happen more often? Colleagues and I examined this issue, which I call coincidence sensitivity, in research that took place as part of the development of the WCS. Coincidence sensitivity is the sum of the factors that predispose a person to noticing coincidences—the greater their sensitivity, the more likely coincidences will be reported. In the initial phase we found that people who describe themselves as spiritual or religious report experiencing more meaningful coincidences than those who did not.[1] In subsequent research, the team defined the personality traits that were associated with high coincidence sensitivity. Participants were 280 undergraduate university students enrolled in a psychology class. We compared their scores on the WCS with each of their scores on a variety of personality questionnaires. Five personality traits emerged as potential measures of coincidence sensitivity.

> We found that the most statistically significant personality trait related to coincidence sensitivity was referential thinking. Referential thinking is characterized by beliefs that "events around me refer and have to do with me." Looking for coincidences and finding personal meaning in them represents a form of self-referential thinking.

The next most significant personality trait was "positive and negative affect." In other words, a high emotional charge, whether positive or negative, is likely to increase the number of connections between thoughts and environmental events.

Then came religious commitment, which is often associated with the idea that God intervenes personally in people's lives. This suggests that coincidences may be interpreted as a means by which people are being guided.

The last significant trait was "search for meaning." So, the tendency to explore meaning in life is likely to be applied to searching for meaning in coincidences.[2]

Not significant in our research was "faith in intuition," which involves finding importance in and drawing conclusions from coincidences by means not regarded as rational. We were surprised that this factor was not significant although other researchers using the WCS have found it to be significant using different intuition scales.[3]

Through my analysis of coincidence stories, I saw some other patterns that influence sensitivity to synchronicity and serendipity. Other psychological characteristics include the tendency to easily make connections (associations) between ideas, activity of one's self-observer, and being predisposed to see patterns and preferring certain biases. The situational variables include changes in daily routine, mobility through the environment, and environmental richness.

ASSOCIATING IDEAS

An increased tendency to associate one idea to another is the common denominator among these personality characteristics. In various ways, each of these traits facilitates connecting an observation with a thought or a thought with an observation. To be self-referential increases the likelihood to connect an observation to a comment on the self. High emotion increases thought production, which in turn creates more connections. Religious commitment seeks thoughts and experiences to support the idea that God intervenes in our lives through "minor miracles" like coincidences. The search for meaning drives people to connect their external experiences to their internal needs as possible guides in life's journey.

Both Freud and Jung encourage their patients' ability to make associations to uncover latent information. Freud primarily asked his patients to use words[4] to go from one idea to another idea mentally nearby. Jung asked his patients to hold an image in mind, then to contemplate it and report how it changes. Each of them often started with an outstanding event in a patient's dream. Both asked their patients to screen away rationality and judgment. Instead, they were encouraged to let their minds go from idea to idea, until the starting conscious idea connected to what was an unconscious idea "just as a waterfall connects above and below."[5]

Like Freud's free association and Jung's active imagination, noticing coincidences also requires suspending rational judgment to allow the mind to make connections between what is outside the mind and what is inside the mind.

Björneborn identified three personal variables that increase serendipity frequency: curiosity, mobility, and sensitivity to environmental stimuli. Curiosity increases thought associations between environmental stimuli and other thoughts, while mobility increases the total volume of incoming stimuli.[6]

SELF-OBSERVER AND RECOGNIZING PATTERNS

The basic mental skill that increases coincidence sensitivity is self-awareness in the form of an active self-observer.[7] The self-observer is described more fully in chapter 14. An active self-observer allows a person to have easy access to mental events. The readiness of the self-observer to notice a possible mind-object similarity impacts how often coincidences are noticed.

Pattern recognition refers to the cognitive process of recognizing a set of stimuli arranged in a certain pattern that is characteristic of that set of stimuli.[8] Coincidence recognition relies on being able to match two patterns by storing the first one with sufficient access to awareness to be able to activate it when the second pattern shows up. People vary in their enjoyment and ability to recognize patterns. Those who enjoy and are good at pattern recognition are more likely to notice coincidences.

BIASES

Several biases actually increase coincidence sensitivity. One is belief in the benefits of coincidences, which increases readiness to see them. The readiness to notice them is influenced by the recency/availability bias. A recent event is more available to awareness to match with a second event to create a coincidence. When viewed in time's rearview mirror, events that create a coincidence take on more significance—that's hindsight bias. Serendipitous discoveries in science are recognized retrospectively when their value emerges. And once beliefs are established, minds are reluctant to let go of them. Instead they seek information that confirms their correctness—that's confirmation bias. One must respect the strength and determination with which many people hold to their beliefs, easily rejecting direct evidence that refutes them.[9] Since similarity between two events is fundamental to coincidences, the desire to confirm that similarity can facilitate the person's ability to stretch the characteristics of one event to match those of another event and confirm the belief that a coincidence has indeed occurred.

CHANGE IN ROUTINE

People normally follow a set routine each day. But changes or disturbances in that daily routine increase the likelihood of coincidences occurring. These disturbances can be caused by need, life stress, and high emotion.[10]

Need is the feeling that something necessary is now lacking. Unconsciously, as well as consciously, the person scans the environment for potential sources to fulfill that need.

Stresses in life force people to move out of their familiar routines into uncharted territory. Passing from one role to another, any change in mental or physical state, or transiting from one life stage to another one, including weddings, deaths, births, job changes, sickness, and relationship changes, are all stresses that force people out of their daily routines. Even vacations represent stressors for this reason, but a very mild form. (A comprehensive list of life stressors can be found in the Holmes-Rahe Life Stress Scale.[11,12] Each life stressor in this scale is assigned a number signifying its degree of stress relative to the other items. Death of a spouse rates the highest, at one hundred, and vacation is fourteen.)

High emotion can be either positive or negative emotion. High emotion increases the mind's drive to make connections with other minds and objects in the environment.

These predisposing factors interact with each other. They are not completely independent. Their relative prominence varies with circumstances.

MOBILITY AND THE RICHNESS OF THE SURROUNDINGS

Because many coincidences are formed from mind-object interactions, a person's rate of movement in the public sphere influences the number of intersections between mind and objects. The environmental richness of the public sphere, in terms of the density and diversity of ideas, things, and people also influences the number of potential intersections and coincidences.

Lennart Björneborn, from the Royal School of Library and Information Science at the University of Copenhagen, identified three environmental factors that were associated with serendipity frequencies. Like me, he concluded that a diversified environment (either physical or digital) helps to increase the likelihood of serendipity. The relative ease of traversing the environment and its sensory stimulation capacities were also crucial.[13]

FACTORS DECREASING COINCIDENCE SENSITIVITY

It's important to note that an excess of any of these qualities can actually *decrease* coincidence sensitivity. Too many life stressors, very intense emotions, or intense need can have the opposite effect. Intensities like these can distract from noticing and making connections. Too many things or people in the surroundings can overload the mind. Rapid movement through the surroundings distracts from noticing mental events. Extreme emotions divert attention from the environment and from free-flowing mental activity.

Now that you have a thorough understanding of what a coincidence is as well as the conditions that create the opportunity for a coincidence to occur, it's time to look into reasons why people believe coincidences occur.

PART 2
· · · · · · · ·
Explaining
Coincidence

5

A Statistician's Approach

Mainstream science holds that coincidences are simply random events and therefore meaningless. And statisticians often point to numbers to explain coincidence. *Can* statistics alone explain coincidences? Or does the reasoning fall short?

We need to clarify the probability of coincidences to better understand them. How do we determine the probability of a coincidence? When is it possible to explain a coincidence by probability alone?

When people experience coincidences, they often think, "Wow, the chances of this occurring are so small!" But statisticians generally believe that people aren't good at intuitively calculating the chances. What may seem improbable could actually be very probable. People tend to neglect the base rate. They become focused on the apparent unlikeliness of the event and do not appreciate the frequency of events like it.

The base rate tells us how likely a certain kind of event is—how likely it is for someone to be struck by lightning, for example. In the United States, according to the Center for Disease Control and Prevention, the likelihood of being struck by lightning is about one in five hundred thousand in a given year.[1]

We may be amazed to learn, then, that Roy Sullivan had been struck by lightning seven times. What an unlucky guy! Then we find out that he was for a long time a forest ranger. This new information changes the probability. The base rate for being struck by lightning is greatly increased when you are outdoors much of the time. Sullivan apparently holds the world record for surviving lightning strikes. It was said that he became paranoid, believing that some kind of higher power was out to kill him. Even though the power was not successful, it worried Sullivan and the people around him. Co-workers and casual acquaintances began to avoid him. Sullivan became depressed and eventually committed suicide at age seventy-one.[2]

The personal importance of coincidences in our lives can also prevent us from properly calculating the base rate. Because the coincidence happened to *us,* it assumes greater importance. It feels more special, more improbable. In Roy Sullivan's case, he felt an awful kind of specialness.

There also may be cultural differences in estimating probabilities. Asians compared to Westerners typically engage less in cause and effect probabilistic thinking.[3]

What do these human difficulties in estimating probabilities have to do with coincidences? When a person judges a coincidence to be improbable, the statistician will claim that that the person has become enamored with unlikeliness—and that it's actually not that unlikely.

THAT'S MY BIRTHDAY TOO!

Statisticians who study coincidences generally believe that "ordinary" people do not know how to judge probability. Statisticians often use the birthday problem to illustrate their point: "How many people need to be in a room to have a 50 percent probability that any two of them will have the same birthday?" Most people guess numbers that are much too high. The answer is twenty-three.[4]

The first mistake made by ordinary people is to misunderstand the question. We think the question is: "How many people need to be in a room for two of them to have the same birthday, like my birthday." We assume that the birthday to be matched has already been selected. With this assumption, more than one hundred in the room is a pretty good guess. Why? Because specifying the birthday makes the probability much lower. Not specifying the birthday means that any birthday will do. That increases the probability. So, our first problem is that most people don't hear the question correctly.

A second common mistake is that most people ignore the 50 percent requirement of probability when the outcome is yes or no: yes, there are two people with the same birthday or no, there are not; in other words, random probability says there is a 50/50 chance for either a yes or no answer. The visual image of the answer to this birthday puzzle question is unfamiliar to most of us: out of one hundred rooms with twenty-three people in each, only 50 percent of them will have two people with the same birthday. Most people are not used to thinking of answers to probability questions like this.

DEGREE OF SIMILARITY

Coincidences emerge in the minds of the beholders. Without a human mind to detect them, coincidences would not exist. For statisticians, human cognitive processing errors create meaning where these is none.

We can pop coincidences into existence by perceiving patterns where there are none. When taken to an extreme, this tendency has a name, *apophenia,* which is "seeing patterns that are not there."[5] (The opposite is *cryptophenia,* a term I coined that means "not seeing patterns that are there.") The Oxford dictionary defines *coincidence* as "a remarkable concurrence of events or circumstances without apparent causal connection." We can perceive a concurrence by overemphasizing or stretching the similarities of the events and by selectively remembering events.

Let's examine these two very common tendencies. Just how similar is *similar?* Computer software developers are actively seeking an objective answer to this question. But, for now, "the degree of similarity" remains subjective. Human beings are still better than computers at finding patterns and judging similarity.

Sometimes we may stretch similarity beyond what is reasonable to create coincidences out of two or more unrelated events. We see similarities that may not be there because we want the connection to be there. But what are the limits of "reasonable" similarities? It's hard to clearly say. Similarity between two specific patterns can be judged on a gradient by human raters (and eventually by computer programs). For now, we can be satisfied with knowing that we probably aren't too bad at discerning similarities and that there will always be someone who will claim that the similarity we perceive is actually not similar enough.

The degree of similarity plays an important role in judging the probability of a coincidence. The more similar the two (or more) events of the coincidence are, the lower the probability of the coincidence. Let's say you and a friend meet up and you're both wearing the exact same shirt and pants bought from the same store and you did not buy them together or tell each other about the purchases. The probability of that happening is lower than both of you wearing pants and shirts that are the same color but different designs. The closer the similarity, the lower the probability.

We select what we see and remember. We have to select information from the huge onslaught of stimuli coming at us. Without selection, our brains would be overloaded. We can, and do, selectively remember certain details and then match those details to a current event. If we did not do that, there would be many fewer coincidences.[6] We also would be living in an ever-present now without links to past experience.

Some people overdo this remembering and matching—selecting just the right memory to create the coincidence. Others may be smacked in the face with a coincidence and not notice it.

OTHER FACTORS THAT INFLUENCE PROBABILITY

What other factors could be influencing the probability of the coincidence? This question challenges students of coincidence studies to examine the variables contributing to the coincidence beyond the base rates of each intersecting event. For example, actor Mike Myers was visiting famed author, physician, and alternative-medicine advocate Deepak Chopra. As Mike walks into Deepak's office, he sees a card on the wall. Mike pulls out his own deck of cards, the first one of which is the same card as the one on the wall, the Goddess of Wealth. Mike is amazed at the coincidence.[7]

But this coincidence was perhaps more probable than it seemed to Mike. The deck contained images of Hindu gods. Deepak relies heavily on Hindu ideas for his teaching. Mike knew that. In preparation for their meeting, Mike seemed to want to show Deepak what he knew that might be relevant to their discussion. While the coincidence seemed amazing to Mike, the context of their relationship increased the likelihood of a matching card. However, there were many cards in the deck so Mike's placing this one, the Goddess of Wealth, on the top lowers the probability.

In summary, the main cognitive errors people make in estimating the probability of a coincidence include: stretching the similarities to make the two elements fit, selectively remembering past events to find a match with a current event, and neglecting the contextual influences that could increase the probability.

A BASIC SENSE OF PROBABILITIES

Despite some biases in the perception of the probability of coincidence, as were discussed in the previous section, new research finds that actually people can judge coincidence probabilities fairly well. So "ordinary people" might not be so bad after all at judging whether a coincidence is random or not. Magda Osman, a senior lecturer in experimental psychology at Queen Mary University, and colleagues Mark Johansen at Cardiff University and Christos Bechlivandis at University College in London, have been working on several empirical investigations looking at people's coincidental experiences. In one of the studies, the task involved asking people to record their coincidences for periods of five weeks. The study did not define coincidences, instead it was left up to participants to decide what they considered coincidences to be for themselves. The idea was to look at coincidences in the wild rather than create fictitious coincidences, such as the birthday problem, to study.

The researchers compiled a set of real-world coincidences reported by the study participants in their diaries. They then asked a different set of participants to rate them by the probability of the coincidences occurring, and how likely they were to occur by chance. Turns out the participants were remarkably consistent in their ratings. For each type of judgment, regardless of the fact that people differed in age, gender, or educational background, they gave similar judgments on how coincidental the set of different coincidences were. They also had similar judgments as to how likely they thought the coincidences were to occur, as well as their ratings of possible causality.[8]

Why is showing high levels of convergence in different judgments about likelihood and causality noteworthy? Without telling people what coincidences are, or how to interpret them, or giving any benchmark of rarity, this study shows that people are fundamentally attuned to judging the likelihood of various patterns of recurring events in similar ways. This challenges conventional academic wisdom that poor probabilistic reasoning leads people to misjudge the probability of coincidences. People do vary in the kinds of coincidental experiences they have, and the frequency by which they have them. However, people tend to agree on what makes a coincidence highly unlikely or not. This requires some basic sense of probabilities in the world.

If the coincidence is random, "just a coincidence," then we can dismiss it. If it is not random, we begin to look for explanations. When we sense that a coincidence is neither random nor explainable, we are tempted to wonder about a cause. To want to look for causes is just the nature of human thinking. Yet some well-recognized statisticians want to eliminate the coincidence as a trigger for our curiosity by declaring randomness the fundamental explanation. Statisticians seem to say: it happened, so it had to happen. Because it had to happen, it would have happened given enough time and enough intersections of events.

Because it had to happen, the coincidence has a probability of happening. Because there is a probability of it happening, probability explains its occurrence. But this, of course, is circular reasoning.

THE "LAW" OF TRULY LARGE NUMBERS

Statisticians argue that, even if the odds that a particular event would occur at this particular moment to this particular person are very low, there are so many moments over the course of our lives and so many people on this planet, that even very improbable coincidences are bound to happen eventually, just by chance.

To explain how coincidences happen, Stanford statistics professor and magician Persi Diaconis proposed the Law of Very Large Numbers, also known as the Law of Truly Large Numbers. According to the Law of Truly Large Numbers, in very large populations, very low probability events must happen. To quote Diaconis and his colleague, Frederick Mosteller: "With a large enough sample, any outrageous thing is likely to happen. The point is that truly rare events, say events that occur only once in a million, are bound to be plentiful in a population of 250 million people. If a coincidence occurs to one person in a million each day, then we expect 250 occurrences a day and close to 100,000 such occurrences a year."[9]

To use a specific example: you think of a friend whom you have not thought of in a long time and soon afterward, that friend contacts you. So with seven billion people on Earth and millions of people calling, texting, and emailing each other and millions of people thinking of each other, there must be many times when one person thinks of another who then contacts them.

Using this example, Diaconis and fellow statisticians dismiss these low-probability events as simply random. To them *random* means "meaningless" in the sense that there is no other cause. Some statisticians do recognize that many people do find personal meaning in coincidences even though probability is their best explanation. Coincidence-focused statisticians believe that people just do not understand how randomness works. If they did, they would understand that there can be no meaning in randomness except what you choose that meaning to be.[10]

But can these statisticians prove that there is no meaning in randomness? Despite the statistician's claim that coincidences can best be explained by the Law of Truly Large Numbers, David Hand, emeritus professor of mathematics and senior research investigator at Imperial College in London notes, to his credit, that at least occasionally coincidences can point the way to important new information.

In 1978 the number 196,833 was independently found to be highly important in two very different branches of math—group theory and number theory. Known as "Monstrous Moonshine," this accidental discovery by John McKay, first thought of as a mere coincidence, revealed a deep connection between two diverse branches of mathematics. Like many of the coincidences of daily life, this coincidence called out for an explanation. Rather than dismissing it as random, a few mathematicians looked into it and found previously unknown connections. As these mathematicians show us, meaning can sometimes be found in apparent randomness if you allow yourself to look for it. According to a colleague, McKay's peculiar genius lies in noticing connections that no one else has seen.[11]

How Large Is "Truly Large"?

No statistician has defined how large is "truly large." A strong advocate for this concept, David Hand, does not know what makes a number truly large enough. He is not sure if seven billion is truly a large number. When I asked him, he said: "Maybe." How about infinity? With infinity, the ultimate large number, anything can happen if we just gather an infinite number of events. That would be impossible to do. Since we don't know how large "truly" large enough is, this idea cannot be a law.

Incidentally, labeling this a "law" adds more confusion to the probability nomenclature because there is already a central concept in statistics called the "Law of Large Numbers" (not *very* or *truly,* just large). The Law of Large Numbers is provable. It states that as a sample size grows, its mean will get closer and closer to the average of the whole. It works with tangible numbers. The Swiss mathematician Jakob Bernoulli proved it in 1713.

The "Law" of Truly Large Numbers, however, cannot be proven. Does the Law of Truly Large Numbers really mean that chance is the best explanation for even the most unlikely of coincidences? It doesn't, argues philosopher Sharon Hewitt Rawlette in her book *The Source and Significance of Coincidences.* Here's why. "The existence of 7 billion people on our planet," she wrote, "is only relevant to our coincidence experiences if we know how many of those 7 billion people have or have not experienced coincidences as striking as the ones we're considering. That is, large numbers are only relevant if we have data for those large numbers. . . . Make no mistake: There is truth to the Law of Very Large Numbers, but it can only be properly applied when we have data for those large numbers."[12] And we don't.

The Truly Large Number proposal appeals to those who *wish* to believe that meaningful coincidences are random events. But believing it says more about the biases of the believer than the nature of coincidences. In the end, the Law of Truly Large Numbers idea does not answer our need for understanding the role of probability in coincidences.

FOUR MORE LAWS

As I have mentioned, some statistical laws are not like scientific laws that can be proven. They are more like laws made by governing bodies and enforced by law enforcement and judicial systems. Legislated laws reflect the values of the lawmakers. These statistical laws reflect the values of the statisticians rather than being proven by scientific experiments or substantiated by established methods of mathematical proofs.

In addition to the Law of Truly Large Numbers, David Hand proposes four additional laws for consideration in our examination of coincidences. Here are the "laws" from his book *The Improbability Principle*.[13]

Hand's *Law of Inevitability* says that one of all the possible outcomes of a random event must occur. So, to see this law in action, we need to be able to list all the possible outcomes, like all of the possible birthdays in a year. How did it happen that my father died on my birthday? How did it happen that Thomas Jefferson and John Adams died on July 4, 1826, exactly fifty years after each had signed the U.S. Declaration of Independence? Something has to happen, but why this particular something out of all the possibilities? For Hand, again, probability is the sole explanation.

Then we have the *Law of Selection*. Since coincidence recognition happens after two or more events cross each other, the observer can select the ones with the preferred probability. To make this point, Hand described the Texas Sharp Shooter who fired bullets at the side of a barn and then drew bullseyes around each bullet hole, exclaiming, "See what a sharpshooter I am!" This analogy suggests that coinciders select which coincidences to describe, which, of course, is necessary. Coinciders are likely to select low-probability coincidences because people tend to pay attention to strange events. That selection does not mean that there is no explanation other than probability.

The third law presented in Hand's book is the *Law of the Probability Lever*. Slight changes in analyzing the details of a coincidence can make highly improbable events almost certain. Here Hand makes his most solid contribution. Those coinciders who want their coincidence to be low probability may ignore factors that raise the apparent probability. The process of analyzing variables can be painstakingly slow and detailed but is necessary in estimating coincidence probability. The great number of lightning strikes on Roy Sullivan presents an example of the need for fine-grained analysis. Sullivan was outside much of the time, increasing the probability of his being struck by lightning.[14]

Hand's fourth law is the *Law of Near Enough*. Events that are sufficiently similar are regarded as identical. Most coincidences involve non-identical events. To insist that only those coincidences that involve identical elements be considered would eliminate most coincidences. Instead, this principle inadvertently draws attention to the need to include measures of similarity between and among coincidence events to accurately judge probability.

We need to go beyond these "laws" and randomness to explain coincidences and how they shape our reality. Probability is a characteristic of all synchronicities but not the only possible explanation. A large swath of the public is convinced that they are orchestrated by God. Between faith in statistics and faith in Divine Providence lie many other potential explanations. As you will see, several factors can contribute to creating a meaningful coincidence. To accept the idea of multiple explanations requires tempering the yes-no, either-or thinking and replacing it with the possibility of multiple factors each contributing to some percentage of the result.

6
Signs from God

Many synchronicities seem to have mysterious origins in addition to their probability. The most popular explanation for mysterious coincidences is that God (or the Universe) is responsible. A belief in divine intervention isn't found only in ancient civilizations or in indigenous cultures. In fact, the 2009 survey I conducted of people affiliated with the University of Missouri found that "the most strongly endorsed explanations for coincidences were God and fate."[1] Philosopher Sharon Hewitt Rawlette highlighted this remarkable observation: "When it comes to unusual events, more than 200 years after the advent of modern science, God and fate still rank higher among the college-educated than the naturalistic alternative of chance."[2]

For those who believe that God causes everything to happen, coincidences are all part of God's plan; author SQuire Rushnell calls them "Godwinks."[3] For many people, this belief is a matter of personal experience, as the coincidences usually involve events that are simply too improbably meaningful to be random, especially when striking coincidences happen so soon after praying. Take for example, author Elizabeth Gilbert, who relates in her memoir *Eat, Pray, Love* how she and a friend wrote a petition to God asking that Gilbert's husband would finally sign the papers for her long-awaited divorce. A few hours later, Gilbert says, she got the call from her lawyer saying that it was done.[4]

Ken Godevenos presents the perspective of a person of faith when it comes to coincidences. He is the author of *Human Resources for the Church: Applying Corporate Practices in a Spiritual Setting* and is active in Christian missions and service. He strongly believes that God directs his life, sometimes through coincidences.[5]

He points out that the word *coincidence* is used only once in the Bible and that was by Jesus Himself when He was teaching the parable of the Good Samaritan. In Luke 10:31, Jesus said, "And by a coincidence a certain priest was going down in that way, and having seen him, he passed over on the opposite side." As translated from the Greek, the biblical definition of *coincidence* would be "what occurs together by God's providential arrangement of circumstances."

Godevenos finds support for his beliefs in many stories from the Bible. There is, for example, the story of Philip and the Ethiopian Eunuch (Acts 8:26–40). The Eunuch, a high court official of Queen Candace of Ethiopia, had traveled to Jerusalem to worship God. But because of who he was and the Jewish rules, he was unsuccessful in gaining access to the temple. But he was persistent and wanted to learn more about Him. So, he found and purchased a scroll of a portion of the Old Testament to read on his return trip, by chariot, to Ethiopia. It happened to be a copy of the book of Isaiah (Isaiah 56), which tells us that Eunuchs can also find salvation. He just happened to purchase the scroll portion that reflected his need. Then Philip, the Evangelist, who was nearby, approached his chariot and simply asked if the Eunuch understood what he was reading. Ultimately Philip helped him convert to Christianity and get baptized.

"What a confirmation for this man," wrote Godevenos. "Indeed, independent circumstances are sometimes aligned beautifully. But to anyone who believes in a Divine Supreme Being that sincerely cares for the welfare of His creations, such occurrences are more than mere coincidences. In Jeremiah chapter 29, verse 11, God says, 'For I know the plans that I have for you, plans for welfare and not for calamity to give you a future and a hope.'"

Believers accept that what appears as coincidence is indeed

orchestrated by a sovereign God. "For me," says Godevenos, "God is not just in charge of the 'big events' in life but also our everyday challenges."[6]

Godevenos believes that God acts in each person's life and that coincidences are one way to do that. And here again, we see that when there is an explanation for a coincidence, there are no coincidences.

Sherrie Lynne, a memoirist and Bible teacher from South Dakota, wrote about how the Bible informed her coincidences in her book *Coincide: A Two Bits Testimony*. She became deeply involved with the number 110. Her interest started with finding a penny and a dime both minted in 1957. When placed together they became 1 + 10 = 110. She noticed that in the Bible both Joseph, Pharaoh's dream interpreter, and Joshua, who took over leadership of the Israelites after Moses, both lived 110 years. She then recalled a dream in which she was told that a shirt she wanted to buy cost $110. When the World Trade Center was attacked, she noticed that each of the twin towers had 110 floors. Because she felt that God was highlighting this number for her, she looked up all biblical verses numbered 1:10. She resonated most with Jeremiah 1:10.[7]

Aside from these Christian examples, persons of other religious faiths who similarly believe in a Prime Mover, Original Cause, or First Cause share the same thinking. Those who attribute coincidences to the "Universe" also tend to share this perspective but usually not as strongly. There is no arguing with people who hold this belief since the person of faith can always assert that the "One" has made the coincidence happen no matter what other explanations are offered. Those other explanations are also the work of the Prime Mover.

Beliefs are foundational to our views of the world. Some beliefs are open to empirical testing, not just by scientists, but by everyone. Gravity, for example, can be tested everyday by dropping an apple from your hand. Proof of God requires some empirical testing and also requires faith—belief by feeling, by intuition, by a "sense of knowing." Into the ambiguity surrounding the meaning of our lives, we can project strongly held beliefs. The ambiguity of many coincidences invites the projection of our beliefs.

But we shouldn't be too quick with embracing a coincidence as divine. "Receiving an answer to a request that you made to a specific spiritual being," said Rawlette, "doesn't prove that that being exists in exactly the way you imagine them."[8]

It doesn't prove that a spiritual being is responsible for the coincidence at all. Could *we* be the real cause of some of the coincidences we experience and are simply attributing them to God/Universe or randomness?

7

Personal Agency

It's been my observation as a psychiatrist-therapist that the "randomness" and "God" explanations often just provide cover for what happens to be the real source of many coincidences. Each of these two explanations takes responsibility for coincidences away from the person experiencing the coincidence. Each explanation suggests that the person is powerless in the face of inexplicable forces. Our reality does not work this way. We have some degree of responsibility.

Randomness says you have nothing to do with creating coincidences—stuff just happens because we live in a random universe. You think coincidences may have something to do with you, but they don't. This is similar when God is called in to explain coincidences; you are the recipient of divine grace, but had nothing to do with creating it except perhaps your faith. If you think you had something to do with it, you are deluding yourself.

But randomness and God are extreme positions in a coincidence dance that usually involves, to varying degrees, the person experiencing the coincidence. How large of a role do we play in creating coincidences? A person willing to explore their own role in creating coincidences can seek out the possible personal implications of a coincidence and uncover their latent abilities hidden within.

Sometimes it's quite clear that neither God nor randomness was involved in a coincidence. Sometimes there is ample evidence that the coincidence was subconsciously created by the individual. The evidence can come from several sources: subconsciously registered sensory information, a need for conflict resolution, or unrecognized contributions from the group of which the coincider is part.

During dream sleep, human eyes move rapidly from side to side. These rapid eye movements also take place during waking hours in scanning and exploring our visual environment. Known as saccades, these quick, simultaneous movements of both eyes between two or more fixation points in the same direction can be elicited voluntarily, but occur reflexively whenever the eyes are open. The scanning picks up much information that does not reach conscious awareness. Sometimes the information reaches awareness in the form of a thought, rather than a visual image. The individual might experience a thought popping into their minds—like driving down a highway and thinking of an airport van and then seeing just such a van. More commonly, the coincidence might involve looking at a digital clock during a particularly emotional time and seeing repeated digits like 2:22, 3:33, 4:44, 5:55, or 11:11. The repeated digits seem to serve as confirmation of one's emotional state, sometimes seeming to suggest that everything will work out well. The ocular saccades may have subconsciously picked up the desired numbers to encourage the optimistic feeling.[1]

Supersensitive hearing might be involved in what appears to be an unexplainable coincidence. A man who called into a radio show in Charlottesville, Virginia, on which I was being interviewed told this story. Walking down a street the man felt the impulse to rush ahead to grab two small children playing under a tree. Just as he swept them away, a large tree branch fell right where they were playing. The most likely explanation is that the man heard a cracking of the branch that was about to fall.

Concordance is another factor that is known to be involved in some coincidences. Concordance refers to coincidences involving two people who know each other well. Twins, for example, tend to think more similarly than other people. They are then more likely to make similar choices when presented with the same event. Very closely bonded people may find themselves humming the same tune or saying the same thing at the same time or finishing each other's sentences. While it may look like telepathy, their many shared experiences increase the likelihood of responding similarly to the same situations.[2]

Outside of their awareness people are able to create coincidences to resolve inner conflicts. Conflict-resolving coincidences are usually attributed to an outside agent. But to an outside observer the coincidence can be explained by the actions of the person experiencing the coincidence. By attributing the cause to an outside agent, personal responsibility is removed, which fosters the feeling of being guided and cared for.

What follows are three examples of people creating coincidences to resolve psychological conflicts. One of our study participants reported this story: "After I was widowed, I began dating again. I was concerned with what my late husband would think. One day while visiting his grave, I accidentally cut my ring finger with some grass clippers. I had to go to the Emergency Department, where they removed my wedding ring. My boyfriend and I took it as a sort of sign that it was okay to proceed in our relationship."

She had cut her own finger. But by attributing the cut to her deceased husband, she could feel that perhaps her husband now approved of her continuing to date. She was caught in an inner conflict that put her in a vulnerable mental state. She sought an exit from the anxiety. She turned to a potential symbol in her environment to guide her. While the final choice was hers to make, the guidance seemed to come from outside. She has acted in a way that led to the coincidence that helped resolve the conflict.

The next example comes from another study participant. A man had committed to attend an evening meeting. When he arrived home, he realized that he did not want to go. He wanted to eat dinner and relax. Nevertheless, he dutifully got into his car. He looked at the gas gauge. Empty! He took it as a sign that he did not need to go. He was the one who did not put gas in the car. He resolved his ambivalence by neglecting to put gas in the car.

Psychoanalyst Gibbs Williams, who wrote *Demystifying Meaningful Coincidences (Synchronicities),*[3] strongly advocates recognizing personal responsibility for creating coincidences that are designed to resolve psychological conflicts. He described a third variation on this theme. A young man entered his first year in college plagued by the question: What is the good life? He had reached an emotional and spiritual crisis. He wished for a sign that significant change was possible. He painted a sun bursting with vivid color surrounded by the pitch darkness of night. Right after he named it "The Sun at Midnight," he glanced at the clock. It was midnight. He was comforted by this sign. This coincidence was probably created by noticing the clock out of the corner of his eye. However, it was not until several years later that he recognized his own participation in the coincidence.[4]

Oftentimes serendipities can also best be explained by the initiative of the coincider. University of Missouri information scientist Sanda Erdelez[5] studied about one hundred people to find out how they created their own serendipity, or failed to do so. Her qualitative data— from surveys and interviews—showed that the subjects fell into three distinct groups. The *non-encounterers* saw life through a narrow filter. They tended to stick to their to-do lists when searching for information rather than wandering off in different directions. Other people were *occasional encounterers* who stumbled into moments of serendipity now and then. The *super-encounterers* reported that happy surprises popped up wherever they looked. The super-encounterers loved to spend an afternoon hunting through odd materials, in part because they counted on finding treasures there. You become a super-encounterer, according to Erdelez, in part because you believe that you are one—it helps to assume that you possess special powers of perception, like an invisible set of antennas that will lead you to clues.

Neuroscientist James Austin describes four types of personal initiative that lead to serendipities.

First is blind luck that is completely accidental; no particular personality trait is involved.

The second involves general, persistent activity that leads to finding something just because events and ideas can collide in possibly fresh combinations. Curiosity, persistence, willingness to explore and experiment may produce something surprising that almost any curious someone may discover as in accidentally creating a new recipe.

Third involves that special sort of receptivity that Walpole called "sagacity" or Louis Pasteur called the "prepared mind." This form requires the past knowledge and experience to notice that this new thing might actually be useful, as in the making Velcro. In 1941, George de Mestral was on a hunting trip and noticed that both his pants and his Irish Pointer's hair were covered in the burs from a burdock plant. De Mestral decided to study the burs under a microscope. What he saw were thousands of tiny hooks that efficiently bound themselves to nearly any fabric (or dog hair) that passed by. Luck is when opportunity meets preparation driven by persistence.

The fourth relies on a particular probing action in addition to sagacity that has a distinctive personal flavor: distinctive hobbies, personal life styles and activities peculiar to the person, can lead to special new findings. For example, a wealthy Spanish father with a hobby of learning about prehistoric human activity was digging in a cave with his daughter and their dog. The dog disappeared in a small opening and his daughter followed. She called back to him, "Papa! Papa! Look! Painted bulls!" They had discovered prehistoric cave paintings that were later referred to as a Sistine Chapel of Prehistory.[6]

Sometimes there are unrecognized group contributions involved in a coincidence. When it comes to scientific discovery for example, it rarely occurs in isolation from the scientific community. The agency of an individual within that community determines whether their observations are taken up into a process of discovery by that community. Serendipitous discoveries in science cannot be accurately described in terms of a single individual at a particular time or place. To understand how a discovery came about and what promoted it, one needs facts about the context and culture.

In addition, many unrecognized individuals contribute to the flowering of the discovery. In the discovery and production of penicillin three men were awarded the Nobel Prize in 1945 because large amounts of penicillin were available to treat injured soldiers during World War II. The final mass production of penicillin would not have been nearly so robust without the serendipitous discovery of the highest producing mold by Mary Hunt. Mary worked at the U.S. Regional Laboratory in Peoria, Illinois, where different strains of the penicillin mold were being tested for their productivity. The U.S. military had sent representatives all over the world to find the best producing mold to grow in the lab. One day in 1943 Mary was shopping at the local market and discovered a cantaloupe with a golden fungus growing on it. This one turned out to be the highest producer of penicillin juice.[7] It enabled sufficient mass production of the antibiotic to treat infected soldiers and speed the end of the war. Without Mary's contribution, the discovery and production of penicillin may not have yielded the Nobel Prize to those three men who received it.[8] Without Mary Hunt, there would have been no Nobel Prize. She too deserved formal recognition. Instead, she became known as Moldy Mary.

Individual decisions play crucial roles in creating meaningful coincidences. Curiosity and moving about with some ideas in the foreground or background of the mind generate many coincidences. Latent human psi abilities, generally unrecognized by conventional science, also generate some coincidences, as Jung observed. As mentioned in chapter 1, Jung included both clairvoyance and precognition as examples of meaningful coincidences.[9]

8

Human GPS

Sometimes the source of the coincidence is not only subconscious but also cannot be explained in these conventional terms. Consider this story about the prime minister of England from 1940 to 1945, Winston Churchill. As a lowly member of his high school class, Churchill took a preliminary examination to be placed in a much-sought-after position. The exam seemed to require special effort on his part because so many people who were better prepared had failed it. He knew that, among other things, they would be asked to draw a map of a specific country. The students didn't know which country, however. The night before the exam, he put the names of all the countries in the world in a hat and drew out New Zealand. He carefully memorized that map. The first task on the exam was, "Draw a map of New Zealand." He received very high marks. The test got him into the military, which provided an essential step toward his becoming prime minister of England.[1]

Was that *just* a coincidence? Luck? Or was it precognition, foreknowledge of something happening in his own future? Research into telepathy, clairvoyance, and precognition, collectively known as psi, has yielded numerous case reports and large numbers of well-designed laboratory research studies. Recently the subject drew a strong, positive review of parapsychological research in the *American Psychologist,* a prominent American psychology journal.[2] Psi abilities have been catalogued across the world's religions, each tradition having stories about people with extraordinary abilities. No one knows how psi works.

But most people do seem to have the ability to pick up the information they need just when they need it most. I will provide two examples, beginning with Ruth's story as described by Sally Rhine Feather in her book *The Gift*.

The mother of six-year-old Ruth went into town to shop, when she suddenly had the feeling that she must return home. "Where's Ruth?" she demanded of the babysitter. "She's at Ann's." Ann was her six-year-old playmate. The mother rushed over to Ann's house, but Ann's mother thought she was at Ruth's! On autopilot, Ruth's mother drove down the street, over the railroad track, parked, ran through a gate, up a little hill, and down to an old quarry now filled with water. There at the edge sat both children with their shoes off ready to go wading. Had they stepped into the water, they likely would've drowned because the sides of that old quarry were very deep. Ruth's mother acted upon, and was guided by, some instinct that she couldn't explain.[3]

The second story is a personal one. When I was eight or nine years old, my father quit his job as manager of a dime store to buy and sell cattle in the farming communities surrounding Cleveland, Ohio. He knew I desperately needed a dog, and one day he brought home a six-week-old puppy, black with tan and white splotches, who liked to chew on trees. I named him Snapper, and we became best buddies.

One day, Snapper disappeared. I became frightened and asked my mother where he was. She didn't know and suggested I go to the police station near my elementary school. I rode my bike the usual route to school, cut across the playground, crossed the big street, and pushed the bike up the stairs and the long walk to the front of the police station. A man in uniform sat behind the large entrance desk. He shook his head, "Sorry, son, we haven't seen your dog."

Tears flooded my eyes as I left. I wasn't paying attention to where I was going. I went down the stairs. But instead of re-crossing the big street, I mistakenly rode on the sidewalk on the right side of the street.

Sobbing, sobbing, sobbing, I looked up and coming toward me was a black dog walking in Snapper's sideways style. Could it be? Yes! It was Snapper! He was casually happy to see me, jumping up on my legs, letting me pet his head. He seemed to be asking me why I'd taken so long to find him.

For many years, I wondered how that coincidence happened. Then I discovered Psi-Mediated Instrumental Responses (PMIR), a concept developed by parapsychologist Rex Stanford. He proposed a model for spontaneous psychic events where individuals may unconsciously obtain extrasensory knowledge of events relevant to their personal needs and use this knowledge to modify their behavior in a way that can be helpful (instrumental) in satisfying those needs.

Of the dozen items on the WCS, this one was in the top four: "I advance in my work/career/education by being in the right place at the right time." Somehow people get where they need to be at the right time. A substantial body of laboratory research by Stanford supports this idea of PMIR.

Stanford assumed that psi responses, like sensory responses, function in support of the needs or desires of the person. In serving those inclinations, the person does not require conscious knowledge of the information of the psi-driven action. By being subconscious, an adaptive or desirable outcome can be orchestrated that can be the most efficient way to move the person away from a threat or toward a gratifying situation.[4,5]

Stanford tested the psi-mediated instrumental response model with forty male college volunteers. Each student was tested individually on intentional ("conscious") psychokinesis using an electronic random-event generator to see if they could reduce the randomness in the sequence of random events. A basic form of a random-event generator (REG) is an electronic coin-tossing machine, generating a series of "heads and tails" outputs. Other REGs are more complex. After electing those who could make the REG less random with their conscious intention, each student was introduced to a boring, tiresome task that potentially could last for forty-five minutes. Unknown to the students, the random-event generator was started in the other experimental room. When a student had decreased the randomness of the REG output to a specified threshold the experimenter released the student from the unpleasant task and introduced him to a presumably pleasant task. The students knew nothing of this contingency that decreasing randomness would release them. This subconscious effect on the random-event generator constituted their nonintentional psi task. Some of them, at a rate well below chance, were able to subconsciously create the effect they needed to be released from the tedium. This result confirmed that human beings in the laboratory can find ways to help themselves without knowing how they did it.[6]

Outside the laboratory people are also able to pick up information subconsciously that allows them to reduce pain or increase pleasure.

PMIR is a form of intuitive knowing. I've given the Stanford acronym PMIR a friendlier face; I call it human GPS—the ability to get where you need to be without knowing how to get there. Being in the right place at the right time happens often but subconsciously. Randomly choosing a seat in a movie theater, arriving late for an appointment, following an intuitive nudge, or getting lost in a car—all of these can yield amazing results. Out of the mist of uncertainty, a needed job, person, thing, or idea appears.

Technological inventions have long been mirrors of human capacities; they are ways to see ourselves from outside. Reflections in water helped pave the way for mirrors. Mirrors were early indicators of the brain's mirror neurons that reflect back behavior a person sees in another person. Mirror neurons respond to actions that we observe in others in the same way as when we create that action ourselves. Computers have become models that mirror computational capacities of the brain. Other technological advances mirror psi capacities. Telephones and text messaging suggest telepathy. Webcams and facetime video suggest clairvoyance. The emerging abilities of brain impulses to move prosthetic arms suggests psychokinesis.[7] These inventions could be called techno-mimicry—technology mimicking psi capacities. Human GPS mimics the technical capacity of the GPS systems present on smart phones and in new cars and trucks.

One study participant told this story about their near suicide: "There was a very dark period in my late teens, a confused time to say the least. I cannot explain the rationalization, or rather, I should state, there was none. I couldn't seem to withstand all the suffering in the world . . . and one afternoon, I took my dad's gun, got in my car, and drove to an isolated place on the lake. The intention was to end my own life. I sat there, with gun in hand, without truly understanding why. . . . It was as if I didn't have any clue how I managed to arrive at this moment in time. But, as tears slowly came down my cheeks, I heard the sound of another car pulling up beside [me] . . . and my brother stepped out of the car, asking me to hand him the gun.

"I was breathless; I was totally shocked. All I could do is to ask him how on Earth he knew I was feeling this way; how did he know I even had this gun, and, most important, how did he find me? He said he had no answers. He didn't have any idea why he got into his car; he didn't know where he was driving, nor why he was going there; or what he was supposed to do when he arrived." One mind picked up the distress of another mind and intuitively knew the location and how to get there.

How did the brother know he was needed? What made him make these complex decisions without a conscious intention? He seemed drawn by his sibling's distress without consciously knowing that they were about to kill themselves.

Subsequently, I began to think of this as simulpathity, which registers the distress of a loved one, coupled with the pathfinding capacities of human GPS, resulting in an uncanny knowledge about where someone is and how to get there. Many similar stories led me to hypothesize the idea of human GPS—that we have the ability to find our way to people, ideas, and things we need without knowing how we got there.

Our psychic abilities are likely an unrecognized source of many coincidences. Once science recognizes these abilities a good many coincidences will have an explanation.

9

Problematic Coincidences

Synchronistic occurrences are often presented as wonderfully positive. I include these illustrations of problematic synchronicities and serendipities with some reluctance. Some of my colleagues react quite strongly against suggesting that meaningful coincidences have their dark sides. But like technological innovations, they can also be problematic. And like spiritual practices, they can be distorted.[1]

Choices influenced by coincidences do not guarantee intended outcomes. The need to decide in the midst of coincidence ambiguity opens possibilities for either positive or negative outcomes. The choices involved with some coincidences may be good for one person and problematic for another. And with time as a variable, a choice influenced by a coincidence may be positive initially but become negative later. Other coincidence-influenced decisions may do the reverse—be negative at first and positive later. *So much depends on how the people involved view the situation shaped by the coincidence.*

Coincidences are signposts, not commands. Their ambiguity becomes a screen onto which to project interpretations. One of my patients told me this story. As an investor, he received a survey call from the financial advisor's company at a time he was considering leaving the company. He thought that the company was trying to trick him into staying with them. But the company was simply sending out a survey that happened to coincide with the time of his need to decide. He had made himself unnecessarily anxious because of this randomly produced coincidence.

A series of coincidences helped to lead a friend of mine into a romance that ended up in marriage. Nine years and two children later, she divorced. Grateful for the time and children they had together, she was able to embrace the end of the relationship. She could have decried the coincidences that led to the marriage. Instead, she was able to appreciate the positives and move on without regret.

There is no basic rule on how to tell whether the apparent intent of a coincidence should be embraced or not. There is no advanced guidance about how to respond to a coincidence. Likewise, there is no way to know the *right way* to respond to a coincidence. Ethics, morality, context, imagined negative and positive consequences, advice from trusted others, as well as intuitive knowing all can play their parts in the process of deciding.

While at a conference, a colleague of mine shared a gloriously romantic first day with another attendee. As darkness fell, the relationship shifted into discord. The next day, each of them wore a black outfit with a little white. For him, this fashion coincidence signaled the relationship should continue. For her, it meant the relationship was finished; the mostly black outfit was a sign of mourning. One person's grateful amazement can be another person's burden. The relationship did not proceed.

GOOD TO BAD, AND BAD TO GOOD

Sometimes a minor coincidence can morph into a global problem. Take for example the story of palm oil, which is the world's most popular vegetable oil. It's in half of all consumer products; it also plays a central role in many industrial applications. Its production per acre from palm oil trees exceeds that of other oil-producing crops like soybeans, rapeseed, and sunflower. Pollination of the trees was once done by hand. Its cultivation and resulting palm oil production has reduced poverty in

Malaysia and India. Then in the 1950s someone who had been working with palm oil production in Malaysia was transferred to West Africa; in the new location he noticed certain insects hovering around the fruits of the palm oil trees there. He guessed these insects were pollinators. Eventually the insects were imported to Malaysia where their pollinating reduced costs by eliminating the need for manual labor. But the increased number of palm oil trees and the increase in production has led to immense deforestation and is a major contributor to global warming.[2] An astute observation became a game changing serendipity that benefitted palm oil producers while negatively impacting planetary ecology. Positive at first, negative later.

The choices offered by some coincidences lead down negative paths, but later positivity emerges. A chairman of a psychology department in a major university was forced to resign his job because of an ethical breach involving a coincidence-fueled romantic relationship with an employee. He left town and started a new life that provided him with creative outlets he never would have had in the town he left. After a decade, he was thriving in the new place. After he left, the woman with whom he had been involved continued to advance in her career through some of the assistance he had provided her.

But coincidences can be deceptive. They can be staged to take advantage of someone. I did not record where I read the following story but it stuck in my memory because it was so carefully plotted. A man was pursuing a wealthy woman for her money. She suspected that he was out for her money. He said he owned a rental house in her neighborhood. As she walked by the rental house one day, she saw him at the door talking with a woman. The woman was pleading for a delay in the long overdue rental payments. The wealthy woman heard the man graciously allowing the payment to be postponed. The pursued woman became more confident that money was not his primary aim with her. But he had staged the whole scene with the woman at the door to convince her of his generosity and lack of need for more cash.

FALSE COINCIDENCES

Coincidences make deeply engaging stories. So engaging, in fact, that some people make up stories to become the center of attention. In 2015, the *New York Times* reported a coincidence hoax. In his memoir, Holocaust survivor Herman Rosenblatt described how, as a starving teenager in a Nazi death camp, a girl had thrown an apple to him that landed within his reach at the barbed wire fence. She returned many times to feed him. Years later, in New York City, he met her on a blind date and they married. The story almost became a movie until, under pressure from relatives, he admitted that he had just wanted the story to be true. His wife had never thrown an apple to anyone.[3]

Accidentally or purposely, coincidences can be connected to evil outcomes. The assassination of John Lennon was triggered by a set of coincidences. On December 8, 1980, Mark David Chapman was standing outside the Dakota, the New York City apartment building where John Lennon lived. This was also the building where the movie *Rosemary's Baby,* starring Mia Farrow, was filmed. The movie was directed by Roman Polanski, husband of actress Sharon Tate, who was eight-and-a-half months pregnant with their unborn son when she was killed by the Charles Manson gang. The gang's favorite song was "Helter Skelter," which was written by Lennon and Paul McCartney. As Chapman thought about these things, Mia Farrow walked by. Chapman interpreted this coincidence to mean that now was the time to kill John Lennon. Chapman's decision made the murder happen, not the coincidence itself. He provided the meaning he wanted to find.[4]

Some coincidences can be falsely promising. A person imagines a desired future, and a set of coincidences then comes along to suggest that what they seek is about to happen. And then it doesn't. A podcast talk show host, who preferred not be named, told me this story about a job interview during our conversation: "Coming back from a big conference, I discovered that the person in the next seat on the plane was the boss of the person who interviewed me for the job. For two hours we had a delightful conversation. I thought I had nailed the job. I eventually found out that they had hired someone else."

MANUFACTURED COINCIDENCES

Coincidences can also be manufactured to serve one's beliefs, often to blame the victim. Fundamentalist leaders across major religions often use natural disasters to blame groups of people whom they consider unholy sinners. The Reverends Jerry Falwell and Pat Robertson asserted on U.S. television that an angry God had allowed the 9/11 terrorists to succeed in their deadly mission because the United States had become a nation of abortion, homosexuality, secular schools and courts, and civil liberties.[5]

When superstorm Sandy hit New York City in 2012, the floodwaters were still rising when some pastors proclaimed that God was angry about the "homosexual agenda."[6] At the same time, an orthodox rabbi was also blaming gays for the flood. To support his belief, he noted this coincidence: After the storm passed there was a double rainbow above the city together with high tide during the full moon.[7]

In these instances, religious leaders matched the destruction caused by natural disasters with their own destructive urges, which they then projected onto their image of God. In doing this, tragedy becomes a vehicle for the expression of their belief. Confirming the belief becomes the prime motivator for the construction of the coincidence. For the rabbi, the double rainbow accompanied by a full moon confirmed that his God had approved of his comments.

We shouldn't take every coincidence that happens to us as revealing a greater intelligence.

CONSPIRACIES

Among conspiracy theorists, there is no such thing as a coincidence because everything happens for a reason. Every bad act can be explained by the actions of an evil government, religious group, political group or major corporation. They project their most fervent beliefs into the ambiguity of a coincidence. Their thought patterns darkly mirror the patterns of those who are certain that statistics or God or the Universe explain most coincidences. Each believes they know the correct source of the coincidence. Each believes there is no such thing as a coincidence because the conjoined events can be explained. Once they are explained, they are no longer coincidences.

In the 1960s several high-level assassinations took place: John F. Kennedy, Martin Luther King, Robert Kennedy, and Malcolm X. Was this just a coincidence? Each one had been leading a large movement intent on changing the way government or religion worked. Who was behind these multiple murders? Against the conflict-ridden backdrop of the Civil Rights movement, the Vietnam War, and the Cold War, paranoia about government plots grew, culminating in 1975 with the U.S. Senate Select Committee's uncovering of evidence of CIA involvement in state-sponsored assassination plots abroad. Could some other nation state be responsible for doing something similar in the United States? Or was the U.S. government behind all four murders?

The desire to find hidden truths characterizes both conspiracy theorists and scientists. But they differ in what constitutes evidence. Conspiracy theorists who believe that there is no gravity don't try to explain what happens when they drop a spoon. They find evidence that supports their closely held belief and ignore the rest. Once again, we are confronted with the all-too-common human tendency to hold firmly to a belief despite evidence to the contrary. The legitimacy of any conspiracy theory is a matter of evidence: Are the patterns the theory points to indeed too improbable to be reasonably attributed to chance?

Can a simultaneous series of power grid failures be due to chance? On April 21, 2017, power outages took place around the United States. San Francisco, New York, and Los Angeles were hit the hardest. Each area experienced problems or shutdowns in business commerce. Also, basic infrastructure such as communication networks, mass transportation, and supply chains experienced problems.[8] Is there one point at which the entire grid is vulnerable? Was this a random event, or was it due to electromagnetic storms, sabotage, or a weakness in the power grid? No firm conclusion was reached. The ambiguity allows people to select their favorite explanation.

Hidden in some conspiracy theories is a plausible explanation. They are just theories until an explanation is found. Unfortunately, some of the theories become fixed beliefs that evidence and data and rationality cannot undo. It's amazing how the desire to believe crushes realistic thinking. These beliefs can be classified as delusions. In psychiatric studies of delusions, both reasoning impairments and intense emotions contribute to maintaining them.[9]

DISTURBING COINCIDENCES

In living life, bad things happen. Some coincidences are hurtful, painful, puzzling, and strange. How? Why? Answers may elude careful analysis. A colleague told this one: In December, 2021, in a single week, three of her friends died, both of her sons got Covid 2,000 miles apart from each other, and her dad needed emergency heart surgery. She wondered if there might be an astrological explanation. Maybe there is no explanation accessible to our limited human intelligence.

As described in the object-object section of chapter 3, Elizabeth Targ was studying distance healing for glioblastoma when she was diagnosed with glioblastoma. Perhaps she subconsciously knew that she had the beginnings of the disease.

OVERWHELMING COINCIDENCES

A barrage of coincidences can be overwhelming. A single compelling coincidence can trigger the desire to find personal meaning and an explanation. When the coincidences come in bunches, all appearing to be meaningful, the brain becomes exhausted trying to figure out all the meanings. All this focused mental energy can force the overwhelmed person to withdraw from reality and become unable to function normally.

Here is a coincidence flood that left the person more than just perplexed. One of our study participants reported this experience: "I met a girl at my workplace, and since the very first day I talked to her I have been experiencing a lot of coincidences. When I think about her, the phone rings; it's her calling me. If I'm going to say something, she says it before I start talking, or if she is going to say something, I say it before she does. This happens a lot. She went to my same grammar school, junior high, same orchestra class, and then ended up working at the same place. But I just met her 4 years ago. I didn't think of our meeting as that important until she told me that she believes in reincarnation and that we had loved each other in a past life, love each other in this life, and will love each other in a future life. She says that explains why I know what she is thinking and she knows what I'm thinking. My relationship with her is not going anywhere. She is engaged and planning to get married in 6 months. More and more, this relationship is becoming more mysterious. The last coincidence is that her boyfriend's sister is very good friends with my best friend's brother. I'm starting to freak out, but I don't know why."

Some people make extensive lists of their coincidences, full of details and connections. They know that they hold clues to some great mystery that they need to understand about themselves or about the nature of reality. And they may be right. Some believe that their stories should be deeply fascinating to other people. Some are convinced that their stories are hugely important to humanity.

I have been the recipient of long emails full of these stories. They are often hard to read because they are so idiosyncratic in their meanings and connections. The authors have little concept about how the reader might respond since they are transfixed in the wonder and amazement of their own minds. They cannot accept the basic fact that their coincidences are far more interesting to them than they are to anyone else. They seem unable to relate their coincidence experience in a way that is accessible to others. I am delighted to receive those rare emails from coinciders recognizing my mind like this one. "I understand that quite possibly every person who has had experiences with coincidence or synchronicities views their own story as peculiar or worthy of awe, so I won't trouble you with the details, as I'm certain your postbox is always full with them." Then I usually request that they follow the suggestions in appendix 2 about how to write or tell a coincidence story.

Sometimes a barrage of coincidences becomes part of a psychotic episode. I've interviewed several people who, during their manic episodes, had paranormal and mystical-like experiences while also not being able to function adequately in ordinary reality. Take psychiatrist James Williford who had several manic episodes. He told me when I interviewed him in 2019 on my radio show that the volume of patterns entering his awareness and the frequency of the coincidences between those patterns and his surroundings were directly proportional to the intensity of his mania. The more intense the mania, the more synchronicities. In the depressed states, his mind was devoid of patterns.

During the manic episodes, he used his mind's eye to look at the past, present, and future. Like a video with occasional sound, he could be telepathic, clairvoyant, and predict the future. One day he needed a comb and saw, in his mind's eye, a yellow comb in the drawer of a desk in an office he had not been in. He walked down the hall, pulled open a drawer, and found the yellow comb he had seen in his mind's eye. He requires several medications to keep the mania and depression in control.[10]

Some people need professional psychotherapeutic help to make sense of their coincidences. One final example. A teacher eventually came to see me because she became overwhelmed when she started experiencing a long series of coincidences. They occurred as many as five times a week. Some made her laugh. Others were of the right time, right place kind. Many others were of the it-gave-me-chills category. She began to question her sanity and her long-held beliefs. The coincidences led her to rediscover Carl Jung and synchronicity, and that led her to my website. After serendipitously meeting a stranger in the crowd of a football game who had heard my radio show, she decided to consult me. We met for ninety minutes on each of three consecutive days. We discussed her many coincidences, large and small.

She returned home more confident in her intuition, more willing to engage others in conversation and connection, and more willing to follow the "compels" indicated by the coincidences. The many coincidences had become teachers for her, urging her to become herself.[11] When caught in a web of numerous coincidences, seeing a professional who knows synchronicity can be useful. Developing up-to-date lists of such clinicians and how to contact them has yet to be done. Mental health professionals continue to avoid identifying themselves as knowledgeable about clinical synchronicity.

I have heard many stories from people going for psychiatric help because they are overwhelmed by coincidences. My psychiatric colleagues tend to call these experiences symptoms of psychosis. They quickly pull out their prescription pads. But the situation is not so black and white. Yes, some people who are overwhelmed with coincidences are having a psychotic episode. But many are not. They are normal people who, for reasons that are unclear to them, are being overwhelmed by coincidences. These coinciders must be careful about who they choose for help. They will need a clinician who believes that coincidences are not necessarily markers of psychosis.

Once such a clinician is found, then the exploration of the coincidences begins. What themes seem to be playing out? What messages might be inherent in the jumble of coincidences? Writing them down will speed the process of understanding. Since coincidences are usually associated with periods of stress, high emotion, and need, what were the circumstances seeming to bring them on?

The teacher, who I mentioned on the previous page, had become overwhelmed by coincidences and was struggling with a terrible marriage. A detailed analysis of the coincidence messages freed her to make decisions for change beyond the subsequent divorce. She became more self-reliant and learned to trust her intuition and her coincidences as helpful guides for decision making.[12]

Some people are having a psychotic episode but the coincidences can also be utilized psychologically. In my experience these are usually bipolar patients who are gaining useful, interesting insights but still need medications to handle their mood swings. For example, the psychiatrist James Williford (discussed above), who experienced bipolar disorder himself, reported that coincidences were far more common when he was manic. They disappeared when he was depressed.[13] This observation is consistent with the notion that the more thoughts one has, the greater the possibility of finding connections. Musician Gary Wimmer was diagnosed with a manic episode and hospitalized, yet coincidences for him led to a profound life-changing mystical experience. Although he was prescribed lithium, he did not take it and did not need it.[14]

Meaningful coincidence experiences can lead some people to inflate their self-importance. They may feel they have been chosen for some special purpose and have been given a fuller view of reality than others. And to some extent they may have. Unfortunately they do not recognize that their synchronicities may be shared by others and become caught up in grandiose illusions that encourage them to lecture others about the uniqueness of their place in the cosmos. Attempts to balance comments by others may have little impact on them.

Clinicians are not currently being trained to use synchronicity to aid therapy, although research evidence is accumulating that it can.[15] Hopefully researchers will continue to study this idea and also develop training methods to incorporate coincidences into the therapeutic process.

Some overwhelmed coinciders may be able to find help without a professional. The Coincidence Project, described in appendix 1, is a multipartner collaborative that is working to illuminate the invisible currents that connect and unify us. The aim of the project is to help recognize the interconnectedness of all life through appreciating and sharing coincidence experiences. The project will offer online places to connect with others who are struggling with the isolation that comes from being overwhelmed by coincidences.

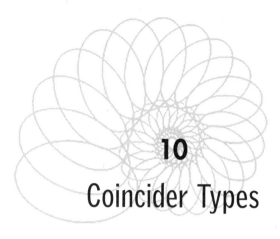

10
Coincider Types

Many people experience coincidences. But not everyone pays attention to their coincidences. Those who do might only notice certain kinds of coincidences. What they notice may be limited to what they perceive as the primary use or the root cause of coincidences. As a result, people who are sensitive to coincidences tend to cluster into one of several types. What is your coincider type?

Generalists are those who notice a wide variety of coincidences—occasional mind-blasters, wide-ranging small ones, as well as spiritual, mundane, irrelevant, and funny ones. Coincidences can be like an ever-present friend—confirming, reassuring, educating, advising, and mysterious. I'm one of these people. I see them often in my daily life and in my practice as a psychiatrist.

The *amazing only* type registers only the big coincidences. They disregard the everyday variety. Jeffrey Mishlove, who hosts and produces the *New Thinking Allowed* channel on YouTube, is one. In a radio interview with me, he related the one big coincidence in his life. "In 1972, I had a very powerful dream in which my Great Uncle Harry appeared. It was so powerful, I woke up crying and singing at the same time. Later I learned that Uncle Harry had died at about the same time as my dream."[1] Because his psychology professors could not explain this coincidence, he decided to become a parapsychologist; he is the recipient of the only doctoral diploma in "parapsychology" ever awarded by an accredited United States university (University of California–Berkeley, 1980). He also told me that he rarely sees other coincidences in his life, although he was the focus of a complicated one involving Brendan Engen, another psychologist.[2]

The *agnostic* are those who pay little attention to coincidences. They may notice a coincidence when asked or remember one when they hear someone else's coincidence story. However, they do not generally register coincidences as something to remember. (One purpose of The Coincidence Project, as described in appendix 1, is to encourage people to tell each other coincidence stories to increase their curiosity about why these experiences occur in their lives.)

Connectors use coincidences to alert them to something important happening in the life of someone they love. This important information is often something that they wouldn't have told them about otherwise, either because they are physically far apart or because it just didn't seem appropriate or necessary to the loved one. By her own report to me, Sharon Hewitt Rawlette, the author of *The Source and Significance of Coincidences,* is a Connector as demonstrated by several of her personal stories. In her subsequent book *The Supreme Victory of the Heart,* synchronicities guided her to a deeper understanding of love.[3]

Coincidences can be used deliberately to connect with others. Social psychology research suggests that perceived similarities between a requestor and the person being asked increases compliance to the request. Shared birthdays, first names, and fingertip similarities increased compliance. (Yes, fingertip similarities were part of the study design.) However, when participants believed the feature they shared with the requester was common to many other people, they were less likely to comply.[4]

The super-encounterers find happy surprises wherever they look, believing they can serendipitously find information treasures in the oddest places. They are likely to believe they are sensitive to hidden channels of information. Described by Sanda Erdelez, the super-encounterers love to spend an afternoon hunting through odd materials, in part because they count on finding treasures there.[5]

Designer, artist, educator, and creative enthusiast Geoffry Gertz considers himself a super-encounterer. He reported the following example on his website: "In the Bushwick warehouse neighborhood of Brooklyn, I was struck by the trompe l'oeil cathedral-style mural by artist Beau Stanton. Serendipitously equipped with my wide-angle lens, I snapped a frame of the hand painted masterpiece and collaborated with my partner Christopher Musci to quickly create a surface pattern from the image and then digitally print it on linen. The exercise meant only for classroom demonstration illustrates the immediacy of technology allowing to swiftly create ideas from an encounter and to quickly translate them."[6]

Super-encounterers include everyday seekers who are developing human GPS-like powers, moving about in information-rich environments to locate something of interest and value.

Some coinciders are adept at using coincidences to further their life missions. They include the connectors and super-encounterers described above, as well as entrepreneurs, teachers, therapists, naturalists, and novelists.

Entrepreneurs incorporate synchronicity into leadership decision making. In his book *Synchronicity, Exploring the Path of Inner Leadership,* Joseph Jaworski suggests that pursuing a deep commitment within an understanding of interconnections and synchronicity will enable leaders to consciously create the conditions for "predictable miracles."[7] He now specializes in the design and execution of large-scale organizational change as well as strategy formation and implementation. In his personal life, Jaworski found his future wife at Chicago's O'Hare Airport by following an intuition to talk with someone he did not know.[8]

Coincidences between *teachers* and students may help to accelerate learning as well as provide psychological support for students. These events are probably much more common than is generally realized by either teachers or students. Christopher Bache, Ph.D., is a professor emeritus in the department of philosophy and religious studies at

Youngstown State University in Ohio. He is also adjunct faculty at the California Institute of Integral Studies and a Fellow at the Institute of Noetic Sciences. Bache, like Marcus Anthony in chapter 3, has reported numerous classroom connections with students. He began to notice that his students were finding pieces of their lives in his lectures. In his book *The Living Classroom*, he wrote: "Sometimes it touched a question they had been holding for a long time or triggered an insight they had been searching for, something they needed to find before they could take the next step in their lives. Sometimes it lanced a private pain that had been festering inside them for years. It was as if their souls were slipping messages to me, giving me hints on how I might reach them—telling me where they were hiding, where they were hurting, and, most importantly, what ideas they needed in order to take the next step in their development. This process, whatever it was, was obviously intelligent and it was obviously collective."[9]

Some *therapists* recognize the usefulness of coincidences to help the process of psychotherapy move along, just as Jung did in the prototypical synchronicity story regarding the scarab that appeared at just the right time during a therapy session. During my psychiatric residency training, a Jungian therapist once told me that "your problems walk into your office." Over the course of my career, I've noticed that parallel many times. Several research studies support the finding that coincidences regularly take place during psychotherapy.[10,11,12,13,14] The coincidences can be helpful to both patient and therapist. The psychotherapeutic setting offers a rich opportunity for applied synchronicity research as suggested by the data from psychotherapy researcher Gunnar Reefschläger.[15]

Jungian therapist Helen Marlo expects coincidences during psychotherapy. Marlo is an analyst member of the C. G. Jung Institute of San Francisco, and professor and chair of clinical psychology at Notre Dame de Namur University. In a paper titled "Synchronicity and Psychotherapy: Unconscious Communication in the Psychotherapeutic Relationship," Marlo described a patient who wanted to be a bird. This wish reflected his desire for a strong mother (bird) to nourish him. The following week, the patient walked to the window and for the first time noticed a baby bird inside a nest that had been perched in an adjacent window for several weeks. At that moment, the mother bird flew to the nest to feed her baby a worm. The event helped decrease the patient's inhibitions about discussing these needs.[16] However, therapists, for the most part, have yet to learn to use coincidences to help patients change.

Naturalists find coincidences in nature. They often hope to use coincidences to help others connect with the natural world and to discover the human kinship with other living beings. South African Matt Zylstra is an integral ecologist with over fifteen years of international experience in research, education, and facilitation of collaborative social-ecological change processes. His transdisciplinary Ph.D. research (2014) explored how synchronicities involving the beings in the natural world foster a connectedness with nature that transforms coinciders to supporters of sustainability. During turbulent times in 2005, Zylstra received the news that a close friend of his had died. Alone in the woods near a small Dutch town, he spoke silent words of solace to his departed friend. With his eyes still closed, something came to rest on his forehead, then another on his right shoulder, and a third on his left forearm. Three dragonflies were resting on him. After a few minutes, they flew away. This was all the more surprising as there were no nearby bodies of water, their preferred habitat. The experience challenged his rationalism and opened the door for his dedication to the study of synchronicity in nature.[17]

Novelists often use coincidences to introduce the story and to move the plot along. Boris Pasternak's massive *Doctor Zhivago* is loaded with coincidences because Pasternak believed that coincidences were part of the flow of life. He reasoned: "The frequent coincidences in the plot are (in this case) not the secret, trick expedients of the novelist. They are traits to characterize the somewhat willful, free, fanciful flow of reality."[18] In chapter 25 of *David Copperfield* by Charles Dickens, David hears Traddles's name announced. Before he can speak to him, David tells his host that the new arrival is probably his old-school friend. "It's a curious coincidence," said David. "It is really," said the host, "quite a coincidence, that Traddles should be here at all: as Traddles was only invited this morning, when the place at the table, intended to be occupied by Mrs. Henry Spiker's brother, became vacant, in consequence of his indisposition."[19] How fortunate to be reunited with an old friend!

Coincidences can and do propel the plots of narrative fiction; many fairy tales, novels, movies, and plays turn on meaningful coincidences. Keep this in mind when watching movies. So many times, the right person shows up at the right time and place. No coincidence, no story.[20]

Some coinciders use coincidences to confirm their beliefs about how reality works. They include *probabilists, flow-ers,* and *godwinkers.* Others, like the *theorists,* apply their preferred theories to explain coincidences.

Probabilists are convinced that all coincidences can be explained by probability and statistics. In their eyes, the misattributions in coincidences are the result of distorted thinking. One is David Hand, a researcher we met earlier in this book and the author of *The Improbability Principle,* a book that lists five "laws" that, in his view, fully explain most coincidences (see chapter 5 of this book for more on these laws). When I interviewed him, he noted the following coincidence. The same month as his book *The Improbability Principle*[21] was published, a novel entitled *Coincidence* was published in the United States, which told the story of a London-based professor who was making a study of coincidences, just like Hand. The female protagonist taught at the same university as Hand's wife. The fictional and real professor shared the same birthday—June 30.[22] In an interview, J. W. Ironmonger, who we met in chapter 3 in the mind-object section and who is the author of *Coincidence,* told me that he never came across Hand or his work before his novel was published.[23] Both Hand and Ironmonger are content to explain this series of coincidences by probability. I prefer to explain it through connections in the psychosphere, which is described in chapter 12.

Psychiatrist Ralph Lewis is yet more certain than David Hand. In an article written for *Psychology Today* magazine he declared: "Understanding the world as it really is—fundamentally random—

can liberate and empower us." To believe that coincidences have explanations, other than being random, weakens us according to Lewis.[24] When I spoke with him, it was very clear that he would be extremely unlikely to allow new information about coincidences to alter his belief in randomness. His responses to my questions indicated that his belief in randomness was as strong as a deeply religious person's belief in the omnipotence and omniscience of God.[25]

Putting God and randomness together, physicist Victor Stenger proposes a God who creates a universe with many possible pathways determined only by chance, but otherwise does not interfere with the physical world or the lives of humans.[26]

Some coinciders use coincidences as part of their state of flow, a term popularized by Mihaly Csikszentmihalyi in his book *Flow: The Psychology of Optimal Experience*.[27] Flow, also known colloquially as being "in the zone," is the mental state in which a person performing some activity is fully immersed in a feeling of energized focus, full involvement, and enjoyment in the process of the activity. Csikszentmihalyi identifies a number of different elements involved in achieving flow: clear goals every step of the way, immediate feedback to one's actions, a balance between challenges and skills, and the activity becomes an end in itself.

Flow-ers recognize that coincidences are more likely to occur when they immerse themselves in the flow and surrender to it. They use coincidences to guide themselves through life. The author and entrepreneur Michael Singer is one. In *The Surrender Experiment,* he explained how he decided to "let life call the shots." He wrote as if he had little to do with how he went from being a college student who almost flunked out to a software designer who is memorialized in the Smithsonian Museum.[28]

Unlike Singer, musician-physicist Sky Nelson-Isaac's recognizes the personal responsibility one needs to recognize in helping coincidences to happen. He learned to expect that help can come from a surprising confluence of events that appear in the uncertainty at the cusp of decisions. He described the process in his book *Living in Flow: The Science of Synchronicity and How Your Choices Shape Your World.* Unlike the majority of authors about synchronicity, he places great emphasis on each person's capacity and responsibility for creating coincidences. In his book, he used many personal stories to show how people may participate in creating coincidences that can assist in the decision-making of daily life.[29]

Jazz musicians, with their in-the-moment, complexly organized improvisations, become pre-eminent flow-ers. Like my friend Charlottesville jazz trumpeter John D'Earth, they find themselves intuitively knowing what the others are doing and what will happen next.

Godwinkers believe there are no coincidences because God is behind them all. Each of SQuire Rushnell's many Godwinks books draw this conclusion for each of the many coincidences he reports. He holds the same belief about his own coincidences.[30] My understanding from reading these books is that the God Rushnell considers to be behind his coincidences is the Christian idea of God.

Robert Perry teaches "A Course in Miracles." He quietly sees God in a special form of coincidence that he calls Conjunctions of Meaningfully Parallel Events (CMPEs). This special coincidence form involves two very similar events occurring within hours of each other. The two events must share a long list of similarities. On average there should be about eight, though sometimes there are as many as thirty. The CMPE is designed to be a comment on a situation of personal relevance. In Perry's view, the interpretation is inherent to the CMPE itself so that two objective observers would draw the same conclusion. CMPEs can provide guidance on decisions, insight into situations, and even predictions of the future.[31]

Theorists use coincidences as clues about how reality works. Jung's synchronicity principle initiated this idea in Western thought. To Jung, synchronicities provided evidence that archetypes (enduring patterns of human thought and action) existed in the realm from which mind and matter emerge, the unus mundus. Synchronicity provides evidence that events could be connected by meaning, not only by cause and effect. He was strongly influenced both by the work of J. B. Rhine in parapsychology and by working with his onetime patient, Nobel Prize–winning physicist Wolfgang Pauli. He applied the findings of the burgeoning fields of both psi research and quantum physics to his theory of synchronicity.[32] The quantum observation of entanglement fueled Jung's notion of acausality. Two enjoined particles, separated at huge distances, instantaneously react to changes in one of them. This instantaneous reaction cannot be explained in conventional causal terms. This observation led to the term "nonlocal" since information seemed to pass instantaneously without the use of a signal or energy. Nonlocal is differentiated from "local." Local refers to a universe in which any signal that is received has been traveling at or less than the speed of light. Quantum particle entanglement challenges this assumption and opened up the possibility of different or "acausal" explanations.

Two psychologists and a philosopher are investigating the connections between complexity and chaos and coincidence by focusing on emergence. Emergent properties characterize complex and chaotic systems. An emergent property can be described as novel in the sense that it cannot be reduced to the properties that exist in the underlying process or context from which it arose.[33] A popular example is the idea that consciousness "emerges" from the neural networks of the brain.

Complex and chaotic systems are examples of nonlinear, dynamical systems that may provide the fertile ground from which coincidences emerge. Jungian psychologist Joe Cambray theorizes about complexity, as does philosopher Samantha Copeland, and independent research psychologist Robert Sacco, who emphasizes chaos theory and fractals.

"A dynamical system," states an article published in the *Journal of Epidemiology and Community Health,* "is a system whose state (and variables) evolve over time, doing so according to some rule. How a system evolves over time depends both on this rule and on its initial conditions—that is, the system's state at some initial time. Feeding this initial state into the rules generates a solution . . . which explains how the system will change over time; chaos is generated by feeding solutions back into the rule as a new initial condition. In this way, it is possible to say what state the system will be in at a particular time in the future."[34]

Unlike the relationship between inputs and outputs in conventional systems, the strength of a cause is not directly proportional to the strength of its effect. A small input can result in a large change in the system. The key differences between chaotic systems and complex ones lie in the number of interacting parts and the effect this difference has on the behavior of the system.

Chaotic systems generate intricate behavior from the repeated application of a simple, mathematical rule. Complex systems generate intricate behavior from simple interactions between large numbers of subunits that feedback into the behavior of the parts.[35]

New properties may emerge from complex systems, which seem to function at the edges between order and chaos. Chaotic systems may give rise to fractals, which are repetition of the same pattern on different scales or magnitudes. The patterns appear to be the same shape but differ in size.[36] For an excellent introduction to fractals please see psychologist Terry Marks-Tarlow's "A Fractal Epistemology for Transpersonal Psychology."[37] Cambray believes the fluid state between order and disorder is filled with creative potential, yet is also potentially dangerous. Too much chaos may lead to psychotic thinking. Structure grounds emerging creativity. Too much structure leads to rigidity since emergence requires flexibility in a system to reconfigure. As Robert Frost wrote: "You have freedom when you're easy in your harness." Complex systems can exhibit self-organization—the system spontaneously orders itself without external control. The emergent property of self-organization may result in synchronicity.[38]

Samantha Copeland[39] suggests the serendipity in scientific discovery also emerges from the fluid state between the structure of wisdom, skill, and knowledge and the unpredictability of chance, luck, and randomness.

Psychologist Robert Sacco investigates the relationship between fractal symmetry and synchronicity. He uses birthdate as the temporal location to predict fractal correlations that become synchronicities later in life. While exact fractals are built by repeating a pattern at different sizes, synchronicities are related to "statistical" fractals that introduce randomness into their construction so that the elements of the coincidence are not exact repetitions. Sacco proposes that because chaos can create fractals, chaos theory can help explain some synchronicities.[40]

A subset of theoreticians are the *serialiers,* those who are attuned to long sequences of repeated patterns, which some believe may provide clues to how reality works. Psychologist Gary Schwartz, whom we met in the seriality section of chapter 3, sees himself as a Master of Serial Coincidences. His book, *Super Synchronicity: Where Science and Spirit Meet,* details his many synchronicities involving the number eleven, ravens, ducks, and more. In it, he proposed a Quantum Synchronicity Theory that, he believes, provides clues to how reality works.[41]

The *number followers,* a subtype of serialiers, are intently focused on specific numbers that have become meaningful to them—23 and 11:11 seem to be favorites. For some, clusters of numbers indicate underlying realities or codes. The number twenty-three has captured the imagination of many. It is made up of two consecutive prime numbers and the only even prime number: two. Each parent contributes twenty-three chromosomes to the start of human life. The nuclei of cells in human bodies have forty-six chromosomes made out of twenty-three pairs. Two movies are titled *23.* John Forbes Nash, the Nobel Prize–winning economist, who was the subject of the film *A Beautiful Mind,* was obsessed with twenty-three.[42] I have a similar personal story with the number: starting with my college football jersey, twenty-three seemed to accompany me for many years later.

Ranking the specialness of numbers has yet to be accomplished. Because there are so many numbers, the seeker for a favorite number will find it in remarkable places. How to select the potential numerical clues to unknown aspects of reality remains to be clarified. For some people 11:11 stands out partially because in the twelve hour clock, it is the only time that contains four of the same numbers.

Finally, there are those who are totally insensitive to coincidences. We can call them the *deniers* or cryptophenia thinkers because, despite their experience of a personal coincidence of very low probability, they fail to acknowledge the challenge coincidences pose to mainstream scientific principles.

These coincider types by no means exhaust all the possibilities. Many people experience meaningful coincidences in several of the ways described here. What kind of coincider are you? Knowing your ways of comprehending coincidences will sharper your connections to both those who process as you do and those who process differently from you. Each perspective can inform your own.

I enthusiastically join the effort to decipher how reality works from the clues of meaningful coincidences. Later in this book, I propose the existence of the psychosphere as part of the means by which difficult-to-explain coincidences take place; more on that in chapter 12. Next, I invite you turn your attention directly to your own life. Which theories described in the next chapter resonate with you?

PART 3

Incorporating Coincidence into Your Life

11

"There Are No Coincidences"

The statement—"There are no coincidences"—reveals a paradox at the core of the subject of coincidences. Embedded in the definition of a coincidence—as two or more events coming together in a surprising, unexpected way without an obvious causal explanation—is a suggestion that there might be an explanation. But the possibility of an explanation creates the opportunity for saying "there are no coincidences." Because if a cause can be defined, then it's not a coincidence. Or "it's too much of a coincidence to be a coincidence."

If, as some people believe, God is the cause behind a coincidence, it's no longer a coincidence. When God is called in to explain coincidences, you are the recipient of divine grace. If you think you had something to do with it, you are deluding yourself. "Coincidences are God's way of remaining anonymous," they say. Or, "It was meant to be."

Experiences involving human GPS and other forms of psychic ability appear to be coincidences. But because psi is not recognized by mainstream science, psi events, which clearly do happen, are regarded as just a coincidence. But once conventional science recognizes psi as real, these events will no longer be regarded as coincidences. Except, that is, for the vexing problem of explaining psi events. Labeling them as psi events is a start.

So what remains after all possible explanations for a coincidence are exhausted? Randomness. But in this case, even the word coincidence would no longer apply, as they would just be random events, not coincidences.

Since coincidence research is, in part, an attempt to understand the underlying causes of coincidences, once they are understood, they are no longer coincidences!

Even as God, statistics, psychic abilities, and other means of personal agency are considered as explanation for coincidences, some remain unexplained—without a cause. It is in this residue of cases that some researchers seek an understanding of the nature of reality. Serial coincidences, for example, many of which appear to have no personal meaning, suggest to some that there is an underlying pattern to reality that is being hinted at.

Paul Kammerer, the Viennese biologist mentioned earlier, attempted to systematize his observations of these series and to develop explanations for how they occur within the limits of current scientific knowledge. He proposed that information could not be destroyed. The longer a system stays together, every part within and surrounding it gains the stamp of the system. When the system does break apart, the broken pieces carry with them the marks of the original system. One way to create coincidences comes from their constant motion; the parts can run into each other. Using the idea that like attracts like, similar parts of the same system come together to create a coincidence series. Kammerer believed that our environment holds limitless amounts of information that is in constant motion and mostly outside of our ability to perceive it.[1]

Jung discounted this theory but was able to use Kammerer's suggestion of a yet-to-be defined cause as support for his acausal synchronicity principle.[2]

Psychologist Gary Schwartz offered a comprehensive list of explanations for long strings of coincidences extending from probability to One Mind, the idea that our individual minds are part of a greater consciousness, in his book, *Super Synchronicity*.[3] He then concluded with a "Quantum based synchronicity" theory that is built upon the supposition that the waves of quantum particles are "real as steel," which was suggested to him by Victor Stenger's work *Quantum Gods: Creation, Chaos, and the Search for Cosmic Consciousness.*[4] In his book, Stenger addressed the well-known wave-particle duality that suggests that quantum particles can exist either in the form of a wave or a particle. Rather than being an alternate state from particles, he asserted that the waves of the particle-wave duality are descriptions of the behavior of the particles. The waves carry form, pattern, and ultimately meaning. Building on this, Schwartz proposed that long strings of coincidences are like quantum particles and form a wave with meaning.[5]

I question how a string of ducks can be compared to a series of particles. Their size differences are immense and questions remain about how far quantum theory reaches into the objects of daily life. What then are the implicit meanings of the "waves" created by long strings of coincidences? What do their shapes and motion tell us about the nature of reality? Schwartz has more theory to develop.

Biologist Rupert Sheldrake suggests that self-organizing entities follow patterns laid down by other entities like them. (Self-organizing entities organize themselves without external guidance. Machines require humans to organize them.) He proposes that nature stores patterns of collective experiences that help guide similar entities in the present. He calls these habits of nature *morphic resonance*—which are shapes that resonate with the patterns of creatures like them. "Morphic resonance," wrote Sheldrake, "is the influence of previous structures of activity on subsequent similar structures of activity organized by morphic fields. It enables memories to pass across both space and time from the past. The greater the similarity, the greater the influence of morphic resonance. What this means is that all self-organizing systems, such as molecules, crystals, cells, plants, animals, and animal societies, have a collective memory on which each individual draws and to which it contributes. In its most general sense this hypothesis implies that the so-called laws of nature are more like habits."[6] This image of resonating pattern repetition sounds like fractals resonating with each other. Collections of similar, recurring morphic resonances create morphic fields. Knowledge of these fields may parallel the changes in knowledge of magnetic fields that, when they were first observed, no one could explain. Now science has a better understanding of how magnetic fields operate. Morphic fields remain theoretical, waiting for further experimental testing to figure out how they work. Morphic resonance attempts to explain phenomena that mainstream science cannot.

Science is great with machines. Not so good with living things.

Again, a crucial difference between machines and living things is that living things organize themselves. A machine needs a self-organizing being to tell it what to do. Animals and plants use their own DNA and something else to organize themselves. That something else could be the morphic fields generated by morphic resonance.

Sheldrake uses morphic fields as a way to explain telepathy. He studied telepathy in real life, not in the laboratory. As mentioned earlier, his research shows that people who are bonded are much more likely to be telepathic with each other. Because they have so many patterns in common, they share a morphic field that provides a theoretical medium for the transmission of thought. Families, sports teams, and jazz musicians share strong morphic fields through which telepathic information can be transmitted. The fields may take years to create. They exist among any group of people who have been doing things together. The group members remain bonded to varying degrees even after they have separated.

The morphic field hypothesis gives support to those who believe that thought can influence reality—particularly when charged by need and intention. The need drives the intention into morphic fields, finding and creating similar patterns. The pattern of the intention resonates with its pairing in a morphic field, producing an analogue of the intended pattern. In this way, Sheldrake believes that prayer for others can help heal them, and that needed objects, ideas, and people can appear.[7]

All theories aside, coincidences exist, or at least *they appear to exist.* Saying that there are no coincidences stops inquiry. Challenging the statement forces us to make sense of its ambiguity and explore our potential involvement. You can choose the random perspective and, with a wave of a mental hand, dismiss most coincidences as not worth further attention. Or, you can seek out their possible personal implications and make life into an adventure of discovery.

12

From Unus Mundus
to the Psychosphere

What happens when a physicist knocks on the door of a psychoanalyst? In one historical instance, quite a lot. In 1930, the Austrian physicist Wolfgang Pauli, distraught and drinking heavily after his divorce, sought out Jung for therapy. In turn, Jung learned about quantum mechanics from Pauli and how measuring the state of one particle can instantly influence the state of another, a property called entanglement. This idea intrigued Jung, who had already coined the term synchronicity to describe the principle of acausal connections. Could events be entangled by their meaning? Viewing Jung's concept of synchronicity through the lens of Pauli's quantum mechanics led Jung and Pauli to conceive of the *unus mundus,* a medieval mystical phrase meaning "one world," which would have no restrictions with regard to time and space further expanding the idea of One Mind. This lack of restriction with regard to time and space also characterizes quantum field theories, which are often described as nonlocal as in particle entanglement. The events cannot be explained by standard cause and effect.

UNUS MUNDUS

Jung fought fiercely against the Western world's reliance on this exclusive belief in cause and effect. "The causalism that underlies our scientific

111

views of the world breaks everything down into individual processes which it punctiliously tries to isolate from all other parallel processes. This tendency is absolutely necessary if we are to regain reliable knowledge of the world, but philosophically it has the disadvantage of breaking up, or obscuring, the universal interrelationship of events so that recognition of the greater relationship, i.e. of the unity of the world, becomes more and more difficult." He used the term *unus mundus* for this unity.[1]

In the unus mundus Jung believed there were psychoid (psyche-like, mind-like) elements. Among the psychoid inhabitants of the unus mundus are what Jung called archetypes, which are neither matter nor mental. They are invisible forms that guide "our imagination, perception, and thinking." Under certain conditions (life stressors, high emotion, and need), archetypes are "constellated" or activated. These activated archetypes link the mind and object components of a coincidence in ways that are associated in time—not caused in the conventional sense but connected by the meaning each incident has in common with the archetype. The activated archetype is correlated with the occurrence of the meaningful coincidence. This co-occurrence suggests a causal connection. Jung introduced a new form of cause—the activated archetype "caused" the co-occurrence of the two meaning-related incidents, a synchronicity.

For Jungian psychology, the fundamental archetypes include Persona, the masks we present to other people socially; Shadow, all that is undesirable to society and to ourselves: greed, hate, aggression, lust; Anima/Animus, the feminine in men and the masculine in women; and Self, the integration of conscious ego, the Anima/Animus, the Persona and the Shadow—the aim of individuation/self-actualizing.

More commonly recognized archetypes include Mother, Father, King, Queen, Wise One, Fool, Magician, and Trickster. The predominantly negative archetypes include Guilt, Shame, Death, Violence, War, Prejudice, Ignorance, Tyranny, Cruelty, Slavery, Lying, Corruption, and Domination of the Rich over the Poor. Awareness of and working through of negative archetypes—the Shadow—are essential for one's personal and social evolution, said Jung.[2]

Jungians sometimes define a coincidence as a synchronicity if it helps the person with individuation. Said Jung: "I use the term 'individuation' to denote the process by which a person becomes a psychological 'in-dividual,' that is, a separate, indivisible unity or 'whole.'"[3] Individuation also suggests another form of explanation—that purpose is a form of cause that pulls people into their futures. So many coincidences appear ready to help people on their ways through life—in relationships, jobs, finances, health, and psychological and spiritual development. Coincidences may help people clarify their purpose in life.

ONE MIND

A modern proponent of the unus mundus is physician and author Larry Dossey. In his book *One Mind,* Dossey gathered considerable evidence that suggests human minds are not contained within our skulls. This evidence comes from mystical experiences, near death experiences, reincarnation memories, distance healing research, and precognition reports.[4] In *Irreducible Mind,* University of Virginia research professor Edward Kelly and colleagues amassed a huge amount of research evidence to suggest that each human mind is part of a greater mind.[5]

This "mind" of which each individual mind is a part has been given many names: the Universe, Source, Consciousness, Oversoul, nonlocal mind, Universal Mind, Mind-at-large, subliminal mind, Big Mind, supra-consciousness, holographic realm, Transcendent Mind, and of course God, though the noun God tends to be avoided by those who do not want to personify consciousness as male oneness. The use of *mind* alone underplays emotion. A more accurate name would be Universal Mind-Heart.

Each of these names generally implies that the human mind has the capacity to extend well beyond the conventional notions of time and space. Taken to their limits, human minds have the potential to be omniscient—able to know the past, the future, and all that is happening in the present. It is infinite in space and eternal in time, able to be instantaneously anywhere in our vast, rapidly expanding universe.

We have difficulty describing what this big consciousness is because we are "in it" and because of the limits of language. Humans are like tadpoles in water unable to distinguish themselves from the medium in which they are immersed. But some people become like frogs, able to sit beside the pond and get a better look at Consciousness. Perhaps we humans can collectively develop a meta-consciousness that can observe Consciousness much as individual minds can "step back" to observe their own minds with their self-observers. The meta-consciousness I call the collective self-observer is to be visited after chapter 14.

Many, many people have had the experience of Oneness and sensed infinity and eternity. I've had glimpses of it myself. Infinity spread out from my eyes in all directions with my mind the center of an expanding circle. I was able to look toward infinity, but I did not see infinity. I recognize the limits of all my senses, including the reach of my own consciousness.

Extraordinary coincidences raise more modest speculations about Consciousness. They suggest that under circumstances that often include need, stress, and high emotion, people find ways to access information that is usually not accessible to them. Intense need can drive human minds to reach beyond their conventional capacities. We have all heard or read stories about someone using some superhuman strength to raise a car to free a trapped person.[6]

How do minds reach beyond their conventional capacities and where do they reach for it? The "where" has to contain the needed information. The reaching has to be done by a mind connecting with the needed information. How does a mind connect? At first it appears that a signal must pass between the person and the needed information from the other person (telepathy/simulpathy) or the distant site (clairvoyance). If an electromagnetic signal were involved it would get weaker with distance. Experiments done in Faraday cages, which are large metal boxes that block most electromagnetic signals, have no effect on a person's psychic ability. Nor do these abilities fade in the depths of the ocean, indicating that even extremely low frequency (ELF) waves are not involved.[7]

Although these experiments seem to disprove the idea that electromagnetic waves have anything to do with psychic abilities, given the state of our ignorance about the substances of the universe like dark energy and dark matter, it is premature to completely rule out this possibility. Perhaps there are unknown information carriers that do not lose signal strength with distance and can penetrate mine shafts, oceans, and Faraday cages. Perhaps living organisms have yet unknown receptors for information carried on these yet-to-be-known signal energies.[8]

More likely, the mind tunnels outside the skull through an unknown medium to the desired information. I use "tunnel" because mind must be "single-mindedly" focused on finding the needed information. The process also resembles the movement through a tunnel in a body of water that permits the single mind to pass through the expanse without entering it. Otherwise, the mind would be flooded with other information.

The fundamental lesson of meaningful coincides is that each human mind is much more connected to other minds and its environment than current scientific thinking would have us believe. By tracking coincidences, we can construct maps of our mind-environment relationships to develop a cartography of the psychosphere.

THE PSYCHOSPHERE

I propose the existence of our mental atmosphere, the psychosphere, that surrounds us like our air atmosphere and in which all beings are immersed. Within the flux of the psychosphere, varieties of energy and information move the way gases, clouds, wind, water vapors, particles, and electromagnetic radiation move in our air atmosphere. The energy-information of the psychosphere includes the full spectrum of human ideas and feelings and behaviors. Just as our living bodies breathe in oxygen and breathe out carbon dioxide, each human mind interchanges ideas and feelings and behavior patterns with the psychosphere by expressing them and drawing them in.

In imagining the psychosphere, I stand back from it much the same way individual human minds can stand back to observe their own mental activity. In doing this, I am part of the psychosphere's self-observer. I imagine the psychosphere to move like water with the eddies and currents of rivers, the heavy calm of lakes, the unbridled power of oceans, the flat splashiness of puddles, and the drip of rain and tears and sweat.

Critics object to this characterization of the psychosphere. They exclaim: "Projection! You are projecting human characteristics onto this made-up mystery." My critics are correct! I am projecting the idea of an individual mind onto this mystery. In psychopathology to project is to put one's own mind into the mind of the other and then act as if the other is functioning with those thoughts and feelings. In normal thinking, projection can be imagining yourself in the mind of the other—an attempt at intellectual-emotional empathy. Since the psychosphere includes our collective mind, it should be imagined to include the basic qualities of our individual minds as well as the consciousness of animals, plants, and fungi, which are neither animal or plant.

I am by no means the first to propose the existence of the psychosphere. The psychiatrist Ian Stevenson had a different name for it. In an attempt to explain how reincarnation works he coined the term *psychophore,* meaning "soul-bearer," to refer to the means by which personal consciousness passes from one life to the next. Stevenson's best reincarnation cases suggest some connection between the past and the present personalities. These personality similarities are not explainable as memories of those personalities still in the minds of living persons, nor by information in the public records of them still available, nor by telepathy, nor clairvoyance. The psychophore would be the means of conveyance of the personal consciousness from someone who has died to someone else being born.[9]

Another precursor of what I call the psychosphere was proposed by the physician Lewis Thomas. He also believed that consciousness was preserved after death. Since nature tends to preserve valuable traits that contribute to survival, individual consciousness would be recycled through what he called the *biospherical nervous system* after physical death.[10]

The French philosopher and Jesuit priest Teilhard de Chardin and the biogeochemist Vladimir Vernadsky called it the *noosphere,* which means "the sphere of mind." To them the noosphere emerges from the biosphere. The biosphere is made up of the parts of the Earth where life exists. The biosphere extends from the deepest root systems of trees, to the dark environment of ocean trenches, to lush rain forests, and high mountaintops.[11] Scientists describe the Earth in terms of spheres. The solid surface layer of the Earth is the lithosphere. The atmosphere is the layer of air that stretches above the lithosphere. The Earth's water—on the surface, in the ground, and in the air—makes up the hydrosphere. The noosphere is a part of nature just as are the lithosphere, hydrosphere, atmosphere, and biosphere. For Teilhard social phenomena contribute to the noosphere and include legal, educational, religious, research, industrial, and technological systems. The noosphere emerges through, and is constituted by, the interaction of human minds.[12]

The internet mirrors the memory capacities of the psychosphere through the apt metaphor of storing information in the cloud. It includes our collective consciousness, which is composed of ideas and values and images accessible to wide ranges of people. In sociology the collective consciousness refers to the ideas carried by institutions that hold societies together. The state fosters patriotism and nationalism. News and popular media spread ideas and practices from how to dress, how to vote, how to date, and how to be married. Education often molds people into compliant citizens. The police and judiciary shape notions of right and wrong, and direct behavior through threat of or actual physical force. Rituals that serve to reaffirm the collective conscious include parades and holidays, sporting events, weddings, and shopping.[13] The gradations of consciousness of animals, trees, fungi, and plants are part of the collective consciousness.

Theosophists have long had their own name for the memory aspect of the psychosphere—the Akashic Record, which is seen as a compendium of all human events, thoughts, words, emotions, and intent ever to have occurred in the past, present, or future.[14] It is said to be accessed by savants, some mediums, and everyday people under facilitating circumstances like need, life stress, and high emotion. In other words, sometimes through coincidences.

MIND ECOLOGY

The anthropologist Gregory Bateson proposed that minds dwell in systems; they are part of nature and not separate from it. "The individual mind," he wrote, "is immanent [exists] but not only in the body. It is immanent also in the pathways and messages outside the body; and there is a larger Mind of which the individual mind is only a sub-system."[15]

Each person may seem to be an island in a vast sea of other islands. However, as islands are connected by the seabed from which they all emerge, human beings are also connected through the psychosphere. Human beings did not create themselves. We are products of biology and society. Minds shape other minds. Relationships create self-identities. Human minds are shaped by personal bodies, personal brains, families, social groups, social organizations, geography, architecture, plants, and animals. We have emerged from a common ground.

Context influences human minds. People change their ideas, feelings, and behaviors when placed in different social and natural environments, whether it's walking along a beach by the sea or taking a psychedelic in a noisy, crowded party. The same person, different mind.

Social isolation and solitary confinement can radically change mind function. As a punishment for being different, some societies shun specific individuals or members of specific groups. Prisoners placed in solitary confinement often lose contact with themselves through lack of contact with others. Some literally lose their minds.[16]

Most people are convinced that all their thoughts, beliefs, and feelings are exclusively "theirs." The existence of the psychosphere suggests that many of our thoughts, feelings, and beliefs enter each mind without recognizing them as primarily coming from the turbulent melee of psychospheric churning. Each person is then challenged to distinguish personal mental events from those in the surrounding psychosphere.[17]

Mind ecology provides the platform upon which the psychosphere can be conceptualized.

SIMULTANEOUS DISCOVERIES ILLUSTRATE OUR GROUP MIND

Scientists, inventors, and artists often make the same discovery at about the same time without having communicated with one another. The list of examples includes the 1858 announcement of the discovery of evolution by Charles Darwin and Alfred Wallace, and the same-day arrival on February 14, 1876, at the U.S. Patent Office of the dual applications for patents by the inventors of the telephone, Alexander Graham Bell and Elisha Gray.

As described previously, a comprehensive list of simultaneous discoveries was put together in 1922. The authors, William F. Ogburn and Dorothy Thomas, found 148 major scientific discoveries made by two or more people around the same time. They suggested that every generation produces curious, intelligent, motivated individuals who try to shed light on a mystery and help make life easier for others. By integrating the products of previous thinkers with their current knowledge and enthusiasm, they lead the rest of us to the next discovery.[18] They seem to be tuned in to the evolving edge of our collective consciousness in the psychosphere. Author Elizabeth Gilbert, mentioned earlier, has a similar take on the writing process, which she explains in her book *Big Magic*. She talks about how ideas for books exist on their own and she has to court them, in a sense, and she tells an uncanny story of courting an idea and losing it, only to have an acquaintance write an almost identical story. She believes that ideas visit an author, and if the author does not take them up, they move on to someone else.[19]

To bring the story closer to home, I was having coffee with a few friends at a local coffeehouse when I met a woman who had been a literary agent in New York City. In recounting the struggles of writers, she said: "One time five different authors sent me book proposals centered on the same specific idea," she said. "Each one asked me to be sure not to tell anyone else about this idea." This is a perfect example of the zeitgeist, ideas floating around in the air, floating in particular areas of our group mind, our collective conscious. They are like information-rich fish zipping around in the psychosphere ready for someone to reach up and reel them in.

In this quiet maelstrom of idea energetics in the psychosphere comes a simple basic principle: if I am thinking it, someone else is also thinking it. I invented the word *simulpathity* in 2014 and two years later a short film by the same name with a very similar meaning appeared on Vimeo.[20] I contacted the filmmaker. He had not read anything of mine. He had come to the word independently.

Each of us is not an island. Our minds are connected in ways that coincidences are helping us to understand. Our mental atmosphere, the psychosphere, is the medium through which we exchange energy and information. We "breathe in" energy-information, and we "breathe out" energy-information. The collective conscious exists within the psychosphere.

AS ABOVE, SO BELOW

Hermes Trismegistus, thought to be an ancient Egyptian philosopher, wrote "That which is Below corresponds to that which is Above, and that which is Above corresponds to that which is Below." The phrase has been summarized as "As above, so below."

Consider for a moment, the spectrum of brain waves as the "below." Brain waves are electromagnetic currents generated by our brains that can be measured by electroencephalography (EEG). These currents range across a spectrum from about 4 Hz to 60 Hz. Hertz (Hz) refers to the number of cycles per second. A cycle in 1 second would be 1 Hertz, 100 cycles in a second is 100 Hertz. The first human EEG recording was obtained by Hans Berger in 1924.

Now let's consider the "above." The ionosphere begins about forty miles above the Earth's surface. It contains ions, which are negatively and positively charged particles created by solar winds. Between the Earth's surface and the ionosphere is an electromagnetic cavity. The lightning that frequently occurs in this cavity generates electromagnetic currents. These currents bounce between the edge of the ionosphere and the Earth's surface. The currents range across a spectrum from about 4 Hz to 60 Hz. These waves are called the Schumann resonances.

The human EEG and the Schumann resonances occupy a similar portion of the electromagnetic spectrum. As with many coincidences, the similarity between these two spectra suggests that there is a link between them. We just don't know what it is . . . yet. Perhaps because our minds evolved within the Schumann frequencies our evolving minds resonated with their surroundings.

Within this similarity between the two wave spectra lies another intriguing coincidence. Meditation, relaxed states, and creative states—as well as the transition between sleep and wakefulness—are characterized by EEG frequencies around 4–8 Hz. During these states our minds tend to have no more than a tenuous connection to ordinary reality. We are "up in the air."

The fundamental frequency of the Schumann resonances is 7.83 Hz. The fundamental frequency is the lowest frequency of its periodic waveforms. The wavelength of this fundamental frequency is equal to the circumference of the Earth. So, the fundamental frequency of the Schumann resonance falls within the range of the meditative, creative, and relaxed states of the human brain. Is this just a coincidence?[21]

I don't think so. These are clues to how our minds operate within the psychosphere.

EVIDENCE FROM DAILY LIFE

The evidence for individual minds being part of larger minds is right in front of us. We need to look no further than our daily life interactions with the people and things around us. If we are fortunate, there are people around us who can calm us down or excite us. What they say and do for and to us influences how our minds operate. These external minds become part of our minds. Grief, which is the loss of a crucial being, not only affects brain function but also our self-identity. The brain's neural circuits that represented that other being are no longer being stimulated by that person's real-life existence. Like a phantom limb, the brain tries to act as if that person is there but is not. The mind has lost a part of its future.

The massive involvement of technology in human minds has substituted individual mental functions for its own remembering functions. Minds no longer hold phone numbers or need to figure out directions using a paper map. The load of information that potentially streams through each cellphone- and internet-connected mind far exceeds any previous interactions between a single mind and external information flow. The increasing number of mind-media coincidences suggests that, in some ways, human minds are becoming nodes in the vast internet connectivity.[22] Our information access on the internet shows yet more clearly that the skull can no longer be considered the limits of the mind.

The theorizing coinciders described earlier will continue to plow their conceptual territories to uncover possible explanations for coincidences. Like other synchronicity and serendipity speculators, they tend to assume that each coincidence has the same explanation, rather than each one having multiple factors contributing to its explanations with one or two factors dominating. The psychosphere offers partial explanations for low probability coincidences, the ones that are difficult to explain in generally accepted ways. The next chapter presents six coincidences that escape conventional explanations and require the existence of something just beginning to be explored—our mental atmosphere. The sixth coincidence involving the sun and the moon seems to go beyond psychospheric explanations.

13

Six Puzzling Cases

I've sketched a spectrum of possible explanations for coincidences. As mentioned previously, the opposite ends of this spectrum are probability and God. However, they are not necessarily mutually exclusive, although proponents of each conceptualize them as polar opposites. In my view, all coincidences have a probability that, at this time, is often difficult to compute but which human minds are pretty good at estimating. Some coincidences can be explained in conventional science terms like ocular saccades and the need for conflict resolution. Others can be explained by psi, though as yet we don't know how psi works. (We did not begin to know how magnetism works until the 1700s; current theories rely on quantum electrodynamics but the complete explanation has yet to be offered.[1]) Future researchers will provide explanations for psi that I believe should include the psychosphere. Many coincidences have mystery wrapped in and around them; their causes are anyone's preferred belief.

In this chapter we will examine six puzzling cases for which psi, whether telepathy, clairvoyance, precognition, or psychokinesis, are insufficient. Stories like these indicate aspects of reality yet to be discovered. These coincidences take place somewhere between the known and the unknown and illustrate how the study of coincidences can expand human understanding of how reality works.

I've selected these six low-probability coincidences because they are ver- ified or verifiable. Three of them have been told in popular media including newspapers, *Scientific American,* and YouTube. Two of them were told directly to me by the person involved. The sixth can be verified by anyone. After recounting each anecdote, I will point out the two incidents that make up the coincidence and note the key decision involved, as well as the predisposing factors. An analysis of the coincidence will then follow.

Burning Lungs

*I received the following email on March 10, 2019, from a psychotherapist and synchronicity filmmaker who wrote: I was visiting a friend out of state at the time and as we wandered into a bookstore, a particular book seemed to call out for me—*Mind Programming *by Eldon Taylor. I bought the book.*

On my flight back home the next day, I got to one particular chapter later in the book. I suddenly put the book down because I knew that I had gotten the information I needed. In the chapter the author recounted a story about how his wife just happened to read on a cereal box that the sensation of 'burning lungs' can be an indication of a heart attack—a symptom that the author had been experiencing off and on for a few weeks. This coincidence involving the cereal box symptom and his burning lungs led the author to go to the doctor within days. That information saved his life.

My father was picking me up from the airport. He started complaining that his lungs were burning. He said it was probably the pollution in Denver and that he was fine but asked me to drive. Having just read that this symptom could mean he was having a heart attack, I argued with my father that we should go to the ER. I drove to the nearest hospital and convinced him to see a doctor. The doctors ran tests and discovered that he was having a heart attack. My father had to undergo open-heart surgery immediately. He would probably not have survived the ride back home to Colorado Springs because his right artery was 99 percent blocked. If I had not followed a simple intuition to pick up that book, I would not have known my father might be having a heart attack.

The two incidents that make up the central coincidence are the reading of a book that mentioned burning lungs as a symptom of heart disease and hearing her father complain of burning lungs. The film maker had made a key decision when she followed the urge to purchase this specific book and then stopped reading when she intuitively knew that she had gotten the information she needed.

The predisposing factors in this case involved the need of this woman's father for cardiac surgery, and her love for her father—high emotion. The life stressors involved here included the change in health of a family member and the very low-level stressor of vacation. (As mentioned earlier, vacations are considered stressors because they involve a change in routine. Many people report synchronicities and serendipities on their vacations.)

The woman who shared this story with me attributed the coincidence to "the Universe." She believes that the Universe is constantly speaking to us, giving us direction and feedback, only if we are willing to listen. Burning lungs is not a well-known symptom of a heart attack. She read this information only an hour before seeing her father. She felt the Universe was providing her with specific directions.

While she felt she was being guided by an intelligence outside of herself, I believe that she subconsciously registered her father's distress at a distance (simulpathity). As she was reading the book, she knew that she had found the information that fit his situation. Finding the right book at the right time without conscious intent is an example of human GPS. Two psi capacities helped guide her to the book— subconscious simulpathity and subconscious human GPS. She may also have been aided by an intelligence outside of herself. After all maybe God helps those who help themselves.

The French GPS

Philosopher Sharon Hewitt Rawlette recounted the following coincidence in her book The Source and Significance of Coincidences. *In 2015, on a weekend getaway in Pennsylvania with some college friends, Sharon was thinking about her ex-fiancé with whom she had lost contact. He was living in France where they had spent time together. Both the ex and France were heavily on her mind. She admitted that "arguments with my [current] husband had been on the increase because of my obsession with France and my unresolved feelings about my ex-fiancé."*

As she and one of her friends were searching for a supermarket to buy provisions for their evening meal, her friend, who was driving, pulled out her smartphone and gave it to Sharon who asked the phone's voice assistant for the nearest grocery store. The phone displayed a list of grocery stores in the immediate vicinity. When Sharon tapped "map" to find the closest, the stores it displayed were all labeled "E.Leclerc"—the name of a French supermarket chain. One of the towns was Carhaix, a town in western Brittany, France. Her college friend had never before used her phone for directions in France. As Sharon later learned by reading her ex's blog, he had been less than two miles from Carhaix that same day. The French GPS incident kicked off a month of coincidences that eventually led to a talk with her ex that led to resolution of her feelings about him and a renewed closeness with her husband.[2]

The two incidents that made up the central coincidence in this case were the phone mapping French locations while in Pennsylvania, and Sharon's ex-fiancé's report of being at one of the French locations mapped on the phone that day. The key decision in this case was Sharon doing the grocery shopping, rather than another of their college friends. The predisposing factors in this case were Sharon's need to reach a resolution of an old romance. The life stressors were the arguments she had had with her spouse and going on vacation. The high emotion came from the turmoil in her marriage and her intense feelings about France.

Rawlette attributes the several low probabilities of this coincidence to a psychic connection between her French ex and herself. She was encouraged to contact him because his blog stated he had been in the nearby French town on the same day as the mapping "error" in Pennsylvania. She believed that somehow her college friend's phone was psychokinetically responding to her intense thoughts about him.

In a personal communication, Rawlette explained: "As in the PEAR lab experiments where bonded pairs produced seven times the psychokinetic effect of either person alone,[3] I think the psychokinesis in this case was a combination of my desire to contact my friend and his desire to contact me—kind of like a lightning bolt where the charge on each side finds the most direct way of neutralizing itself."[4] This lightning bolt analogy illustrates that what we are seeking is often also seeking us.

While machines sometimes seem to respond to human minds, the specificity of this response demands further explanation. As many coincidences seem to indicate, people are becoming more connected to their machines than is currently understood. The increasing number of coincidences between human minds and the internet is more than advertisers targeting viewers' preferences.

Rawlette continues: "But the coincidence suggests to me that there may have been some yet-to-be-identified conscious being who was aware of the life plan or destiny of each of us and knew that this particular exchange was vital for each of us: for me, because it led me to research and write this enormous book on coincidences, which I believe was part of my mission in life and which has since led me to other vital connections, including one that is now drawing me back to France."[5]

Rather than being directed by a conscious being, I instead see both people being connected through the psychosphere, their intentions catalyzing their need for a resolution. The Greeks thought that Apollo and his chariot pulled the sun across the sky—a conscious being acting on the world. Later observations were able to confirm that the sun appears to move because of the Earth's rotation on its axis. As a psychiatrist, I look for a mechanism rather than an intelligence. So resonance with a compatible pattern through the psychosphere becomes an alternative explanation. Nevertheless, mystery may also be involved. I deeply respect Sharon's feeling and sense that an intelligence outside of her normal self also influenced this very meaningful coincidence. Like the "burning lungs story" this coincidence charges us to explore further reaches of consciousness.

The Balloon

One of the most iconic of meaningful coincidences is the story of Laura Buxton's balloon; the story has appeared in several documentaries,[6,7] and on National Public Radio's RadioLab, where the girls were interviewed and the incidents analyzed.[8]

In June 2001, ten-year-old Laura Buxton of Staffordshire, England, was attending her grandparent's golden wedding anniversary. She was in need of a friend. Her grandfather thought she could find a pen pal for herself by writing her address on a label with the message "Please return to Laura Buxton." They attached it to a helium balloon that was part of the anniversary celebration and sent the balloon off into the sky.

A farmer in Milton Lilbourne, Wiltshire, about one hundred and forty miles away, pulled the balloon out of the hedge that separated his pastures from the neighbor's. He noticed the name Laura Buxton. Since this was the name of his neighbor's daughter, he brought the balloon to her.

The Laura Buxton from Milton Lilbourne, who was also ten years old, then wrote to Laura Buxton in Staffordshire. As this was such an interesting coincidence, their parents arranged for them to meet.

When they met, they were wearing similar clothes and discovered that they had three similar pets, including three-year-old black Labrador retrievers.

The girls became close friends.

The two incidents making up the central coincidence were the grandfather sending off a helium balloon with a note attached, and a man one hundred and forty miles away finding the balloon and giving it to his neighbor's daughter, whose name he thought was on the note.

Both parents decided the girls should meet; this was the key decision. Without this decision, the coincidence would not have been realized.

The predisposing factors included the fact that both girls felt the need for a friend, with the life stressors taking place including a wedding anniversary celebration, and the fact that the other Laura and her family members were sick at the time. The anniversary celebration and the grandfather's love of his granddaughter made this a time of high emotion.

So what was the cause of this coincidence? A "lucky wind"? Like attracts like? Because the story has been so well documented, statisticians have tried to explain this very low-probability event by using the bell-shaped curve—that this was an event way out in the tail of the curve, in other words, rare but still possible. Even if the winds were strong that day, how could they have carried the balloon to another Laura Buxton one hundred and forty miles away? How did the balloon even survive that long in the air?

For the girls, the event answered a wish each had; it was also a fulfillment of a grandfatherly intent. Something very strange happened between those two girls. Here is a mystery that modern science has yet to explain.

I think our mental atmosphere once again contributed. The predisposing factors opened up a link in the psychosphere between the two girls that guided the balloon to meet their need. But why these two girls? Under conditions we do not understand yet, pathways open up that reach into the material world and guide things and people to where they can have significant impact. The girls finding each other is another example of the idea that what you are seeking may also be seeking you. This coincidence offers another clue about mapping the psychosphere and how it works.

The Silent Radio

Michael Shermer is an American science writer, founder of The Skeptics Society, and editor-in-chief of its magazine, Skeptic. *He is not prone to giving what he calls pseudoscientific and supernatural claims any credence. But he came out of the closet of sorts in an October 2014 article he wrote for* Scientific American, *a bastion of mainstream science. "I just witnessed an event so mysterious that it shook my skepticism," he wrote.*[9]

Michael Shermer was about to marry Jennifer Graf, from Köln, Germany. She had been raised by her mom. Her grandfather, Walter, was the closest father figure she had growing up, but he died when she was sixteen. His 1978 Philips transistor radio was part of a collection of his belongings that Jennifer had kept, and which Michael had set out to bring back to life after decades of muteness. Unsuccessfully. So he put the radio at the back of a desk drawer in their bedroom.

Michael and Jennifer's marriage took place on June 25, 2014, in Michael's home. Being nine thousand kilometers from family, friends, and home, Jennifer was feeling lonely. She had wanted her grandfather to give her away.

Then, as the ceremony was about to begin, they heard music playing in the bedroom. They followed the sound to the desk in their bedroom. When Jennifer opened the desk drawer and pulled out her grandfather's transistor radio, it was playing a love song. "My grandfather is here with us," Jennifer said, tearfully. "I'm not alone."

Later that night they fell asleep to the sound of classical music coming from Walter's radio. The radio stopped working the next day and has remained silent ever since.

Two incidents make up the central coincidence, one involving mind: Jennifer wanting the presence of her deceased, beloved grandfather at her wedding; the other involving an object, her grandfather's silent old radio, which started playing romantic music as the wedding was about to begin.

The key decision was Michael's attempt to fix the radio, but failing to do so.

The predisposing factor was the need for the presence of Jennifer's grandfather, the life stressor was the marriage itself, and the high emotion came from both Jennifer's love for her grandfather and the wedding excitement.

What woke up the dormant radio? Was it a change in humidity or temperature or the vibrations caused by all the people in the house? Harder, if not impossible, to account for in conventional terms was the timing of the event: it occurred right before the ceremony began.

It is worth listening to Michael's first analysis of the coincidence. "Had it happened to someone else," he wrote, "I might suggest a chance electrical anomaly and the law of large numbers [he meant the law of truly large numbers] as an explanation—with billions of people having billions of experiences every day, there's bound to be a handful of extremely unlikely events that stand out in their timing and meaning. In any case, such anecdotes do not constitute scientific evidence that the dead survive or that they can communicate with us via electronic equipment. . . . [But] the eerie conjunction of these deeply evocative events gave Jennifer the distinct feeling that her grandfather was there and that the music was his gift of approval."[10]

In his 2018 book *Heavens on Earth: The Scientific Search for the Afterlife, Immortality, and Utopia,* Michael offered another explanation. He turned to the sci-fi film *Interstellar,* in which the hero passes through a wormhole and saves humankind by communicating through portals from another dimension. A wormhole to another dimension may be a strange explanation for the well-timed love song—but Michael argued that it's at least grounded in conventionally accepted science. Perhaps Grandfather Walter exists in another dimension, where he can see Jennifer at all times of her life simultaneously and use gravitational waves from a wormhole to turn on his old radio?[11]

I look for causal mechanisms involving Jennifer, the coincider, and the involvement of some aspect of the psychosphere. Perhaps Jennifer's need psychokinetically activated the dormant radio. Like the French GPS anecdote, perhaps the machine responded to focused human energy.

I think her need for her grandfather at that moment activated the hypothetical signature vibration of her grandfather stored in the psychosphere, to which the radio was aligned, since it was his radio.

(A signature vibration is the basic, personal vibration of each living body like a fingerprint.) Or perhaps both Michael and I are correct—that the spirit of her grandfather in one form or another activated his radio at the most fitting moment. More mystery to explore with synchronicity.

Earth Coincidence Control Office

Adam Trombly is an internationally acknowledged expert in the fields of physics, atmospheric dynamics, geophysics, rotating and resonating electromagnetic systems, and environmental global modeling.

In the early 1990s Adam had stage 4 neuroblastoma cancer. Neuroblastomas develop from immature nerve cells found in several areas of the body including the adrenal glands.

The coincidence occurred while Adam was visiting John Lilly, the neuroscientist and psychonaut, in California in 1991. Adam described what happened in an interview that took place fourteen years later.[12]

Adam had received a call from his daughter, then age thirteen. John was in the next room meditating during the phone call. When John rejoined Adam, John said "ECCO says you will recover. You have too much work to do." ECCO was John's shorthand for Earth Coincidence Control Office.

An hour or so later Adam was alone in John's home when the doorbell rang. A physician introduced himself to Adam, saying that during his meditation a voice told him to come to this house and bring his medical bag, which had the old version of ketamine in it. He had never been to the Lilly home before. The physician administered intramuscular ketamine to Adam. Adam did not report in his interview why he let a complete stranger administer ketamine to him. I imagine that Adam thought that this physician was sent by his friend John, perhaps by ECCO. Subsequently, the cancer went into remission for several years until an effective treatment was found.

The incidents making up the central coincidence were Adam needing help and the physician following the directions of a "voice" who told him to go to a specific house with his medical bag. This was a mind-mind coincidence.

Adam's going to John Lilly's house despite stage 4 cancer was the key decision. The predisposing factor: Adam's need for cancer treatment. Adam's stage 4 cancer was the life stressor, and the high emotion was his daughter's love—Adam and his daughter often prayed together about love being the most powerful of powers. The other powerful emotion was the fear of dying.

Adam and the physician had no apparent previous connection with each other. John Lilly reported that ECCO told him that Adam would live. That implies that ECCO communicated with the physician to tell him to go to John's house with the ketamine.

There are many similar reports of conscious, intentional beings in the psychosphere.[13] ECCO is particularly intriguing because, according to John Lilly, this is the lowest control office in the universe. "There exists a Cosmic Coincidence Control Center (CCCC) with a Galactic substation called Galactic Coincidence Control (GCC). Within GCC is the Solar System Control Unit (SSCU), within which is the Earth Coincidence Control Office (ECCO)." This suggests that the psychosphere is also part of a nested series of information consciousness spheres throughout the universe.[14]

The Sun and the Moon Appear to be Exactly the Same Size

There is one coincidence for everyone on Earth to see: the sun and moon appear to us to be exactly the same size. Solar eclipses, when the moon passes between Earth and sun, dramatically demonstrate their apparently equal size. But, of course, they are not the same size. They are about ninety-three million miles apart. The sun is about four hundred times larger than the moon. But because the moon is also four hundred times closer to Earth, the geometry makes them appear to be the same size.[15] Written algebraically, $400/1 \times 1/400 = 1$.

Astronomers say that the moon was created 4.5 billion years ago when a Mars-sized object (or perhaps a series of many smaller objects) crashed into the Earth, sending bits of the Earth's crust into space. The bits fell into the Earth's orbit and eventually coalesced, forming our moon. That newborn moon—a ball of molten rock covered in a magma ocean—was nearly 16 times closer to Earth than it is today. Now the moon is being pushed away from Earth by 1.6 inches (4 centimeters) per year.[16]

If this moon creation theory is correct, then a second coincidence is that, in the broad expanse of time for the moon to reach its current position in the sky, perhaps one hundred million years, the apparent equality in size is happening while humans are around to observe it.[17] The two incidents of this coincidence are the moon's evolution matching in time the evolution of human consciousness to be able to notice the similarity between the sun and the moon. As usual with very low-probability coincidences, people invoke their preferred explanations. Astronomers support randomness, that in our ever-expanding universe, any weird thing can happen.[18] Parapsychology and quantum mechanics offer no clues. On the fringe are hard-to-believe conjectures that the moon was somehow manufactured.[19] I believe that the sun-moon coincidence is there to remind us Earth dwellers to pay attention to coincidences.

THE POSSIBLE OPERATIONS OF
THE PSYCHOSPHERE

These six stories provide insights into the nature of coincidences. The French GPS and the balloon stories suggest a potential principle—that which a person seeks is also seeking that person. This principle is a more active, intentional form of "like attracts like." The sun-moon coincidence highlights the difficulty in solving the mysteries of many coincidences.

Each of the five personal cases suggests there exists somewhere, somehow, something (an intentional being or a mechanism or both) by which human beings tap into a source of help under certain conditions involving need, life stressors, and high emotion. The need defines and clarifies an intention. Life stressors stretch the web of everyday reality, creating openings for new possibilities. And high emotion drives the need-intention into the psychosphere. In the psychosphere the mind tunnels single-mindedly to the needed information.

I suspect that under these conditions the mind becomes less tethered to the brain and comes in closer contact with the needed resources in the psychosphere. The mind then bridges the brain and the psychosphere. While the mind serves as an intermediary between brain and psychosphere, it also possesses its own distinct capacities. These distinct capacities allow the mind to connect body (brain-heart) energy to the needed resonant patterns in the psychosphere that then can feed back through the mind's bridge to the brain for actionable thought that can lead to behavior to fulfill the need. As a conduit between brain and psychosphere, the mind can direct brain-heart energy to other minds and objects through the psychosphere by finding and activating resonant patterns associated with the targeted minds or objects.

How do thoughts in the mind find resonant patterns in the psychosphere? Radios and TVs can tune to selected channels; email addresses, phone calls, and texts find the intended recipient. Resonating patterns of emotionally charged need can pair with relevant information-energy patterns in the psychosphere to fulfill the need. Consider the following more detailed mental image.

I imagine personal energy-information balloons representing each human mind floating in the psychosphere. Each balloon is connected to the individual mind that hovers around the skull-encased brain. Like conventional balloons they can inflate and deflate, and are buffeted and tossed in the ebbs and flows of the psychosphere, each with an energetic cord connecting it to its earthbound twin. When two people find themselves in an emotional relationship, their psychospheric balloons connect with each other. An energetic, vibrating, four-sided figure is temporarily formed composed of energetic lines between each earthbound mind, and between each psychospheric balloon, as well as between each personal balloon to the personal mind of each participant. The conductive capacities of the link between the psychospheric balloons are directly proportional to the strength of the feeling between the earthbound minds. Information can then pass fluidly between the psychospheric balloons and the skull-bound minds while they are at a distance from each other. This arrangement can lead to simulpathity and telepathy.

I imagine that the brain, mind, and psychosphere are each composed of the same kind of energy-information. They differ from each other in their degree of density, the way water has three densities as ice, liquid, and gas. Just as each form of water is composed of water molecules, the brain, mind, and psychosphere are composed of the same "molecules" of energy-information. And just as barriers exist between ice and liquid as well as liquid and gas, so do barriers exist between the brain, mind, and psychosphere. In water, the transition between states requires the input of energy; energy needs to be applied or taken away to create state shifts. By analogy, I imagine that the energy information states of the brain, mind, and psychosphere can be traversed by adding or removing energy. In writing about the relationship between mind and body, Jung wrote something quite similar: "The psyche and the body should be viewed as different manifestations of a single energy and their relationship be understood in terms of the transformation of this energy into greater or lesser states of intensification."[20]

BRAIN AS FILTER

A competing explanation about the relationship between the psychosphere and the brain is that the brain acts as a filter for the energy information in the psychosphere. From a psychiatric perspective, psychosis sometimes appears to be a breakdown in a filter, allowing multiple streams of thought to enter the mind. In some way, information from the personal unconscious and from the collective unconscious becomes all too readily available. For people in various altered states of consciousness the filter between brain and psychosphere becomes more permeable. The personal unconscious can emerge into conscious awareness. How then does this energy-information from the psychosphere enter the brain and then go from the brain to the mind? I have not seen an explanation from those writing about the brain as a filter. It is my impression that they neglect the individual mind itself and think of it as already part of the psychosphere.[21] What's remarkable in the end is that whatever the cause behind many strange coincidences, they are, as I can attest as a psychiatrist, sometimes of immense use to those experiencing them.

14

The Practical Uses
of Coincidences

There is more for us to know about coincidences. But we do know that, regardless of explanation, meaningful coincidences help people to navigate the practical, psychological, and spiritual in daily life, and to inspire innovations in science, technology, organizational development, and the arts.

Coincidences are useful in *demonstrating connections*. The simulpathy and human GPS stories illustrate human capacities yet to be recognized by modern science. Coincidences via "telepathic impressions" are most common among people who know each other well, which includes not only family but close friends. This "knowing each other well" most likely includes deep emotional and physical bonds, which leads to the creation of "tunnels between minds." Like ocean tides influenced by the moon, the movement of energy-information through the tunnels ebbs and flows with changes in emotional states of the tunnel partners. My own experiences and the reports of friends and patients suggest that telepathic connections may be intentionally created, something like pushing a button on a cell phone to call or text someone.

Coincidences also *help in decision making*. Coincidences can influence decisions in many aspects of life including: relationship issues (romance, family, and friends), health questions, employment, and financial directions. Following the stages of change described by James O. Prochaska, author of "Decision Making in the Transtheoretical Model of Behavior Change,"[1] coincidences can play a role in each of the five steps in the decision-making process.

These five steps include:

- recognizing the need to decide,
- gathering alternatives,
- choosing,
- timing the decision, and
- using hindsight to confirm or challenge a decision.

The first step is *recognizing the need to decide.* Take this story as related by Rachel Herron who drives for Uber. She picked up a woman at the airport whose destination happened to be the address of the apartment complex where Rachel's boyfriend lived. Earlier that day Rachel's boyfriend had taken his car to the airport to take a flight to visit his sick mother. She had stayed with him the night before.

The passenger began talking about herself, saying she is in town to visit her boyfriend. She was so excited. She hadn't seen him in forever. Rachel related to what she was saying because her man had just left town.

As they pulled into the apartment complex, Rachel said that her boyfriend also lived out here. Her stomach dropped when she saw her boyfriend's car outside his building. She started burning up inside as the passenger said, "I think it is right here. This is his car."

The boyfriend came out of the building to help the passenger with the luggage. Rachel started hitting him and the passenger started hitting her. Then the boyfriend tried to break them up. Finally, with her heart hurting, Rachel got back in her car while the passenger was kicking her car. Rachel drove off with the passenger's luggage. She ended the saga with, "By the way, I am single now."[2] Clearly the coincidence prompted her to recognize her need to decide. How unexpectedly informative to actually drive the other girlfriend to her now ex-boyfriend's place!

The second step in the decision-making process is *gathering alternatives*. When selecting from multiple options, coincidences can offer new and possibly better options. I was conducting psychiatric interviews via the internet with a patient in Hong Kong while I was in Charlottesville, Virginia. She had become quite agitated but had not told me about it in any detail. Her family took her to a Hong Kong psychiatrist who prescribed a low dose of aripiprazole, which quickly helped to calm her agitation. I had not prescribed this medication in several years and would not have considered it for her.

The following week, another patient of mine revealed her on-going agitation. She was now ready to consider adding another medication. I prescribed the same low dose of aripiprazole—with very positive results. I would not have thought of aripiprazole as the first possibility without its recent benefit to my Hong Kong patient. Receiving the report about the Hong Kong patient provided an alternative I would not have readily considered for my Virginia patient.

The third step in the decision-making process is *choosing*.

Henry Fierz visited Jung in the 1950s at the appointed hour of 5:00 p.m. to discuss whether a manuscript by a scientist who had recently died should be published. Jung had decided that it should not be. When the discussion became heated, Jung looked at his wristwatch, obviously thinking the conversation should come to an end. Looking up from his watch, he said, "What time did you come?"

Fierz responded, "At five, as agreed."

Jung: "But that's queer. My watch came back from the watchmaker this morning after a complete revision, and now I have 5:05. But you must have been here much longer. What time do you have?"

"It's 5:35," said Fierz.

Whereupon Jung said: "So you have the right time, and I have the wrong one. Let us discuss the thing again." This time Fierz convinced Jung that the book should be published. Jung interpreted the incorrect time as a synchronistic comment on his conclusion about the publication that was also incorrect.[3]

The fourth step in the decision-making process is *the timing for a decision*. Coincidences can pop up at just the right time to trigger a decision. One of our research participants reported this story: "Last weekend I was waiting at a red light, and as it turned green, my cell phone rang. I looked down to answer the phone, thereby delaying my acceleration into the intersection. When I looked back up, a truck ran the red light through the intersection just where I would be if I'd started at the change of the light. This was meaningful because it was a call from my older brother with whom I haven't spoken in months, and I've always felt like he was a protector of mine." His fortunately timed call had saved her from difficulty once again.

Coincidences can encourage decisive action when it appears that action is not necessary. Dana Nelson-Isaacs reported the following story to her husband, Sky Nelson-Isaacs, as recounted in his book *Leap to Wholeness*. "I kept getting cell phone calls from an unknown source identifying themselves as our electrical utility company. They were threatening to disconnect our service if we didn't call back with our sensitive personal information. Suspecting it was a scam, I hung up and called the utility company directly. It was the same number, so I figured maybe it was legitimate. After a long wait I reached the receptionist, and he confirmed that there is indeed a scam in which the perpetrators mimic their phone number. I was about to get off the phone, happy to have avoided the scam, when it occurred to me to ask about our account while I had the person's attention. After he opened our file, it turned out that our electricity was scheduled to be shut off the following Monday! We had accidentally underpaid and missed the warning notices. Those scammers helped us out!"[4] Dana had helped herself by following her intuitive lead to ask about their bill.

The fifth step in the decision-making process is *hindsight*. Coincidences may in retrospect confirm a decision or challenge it. A favorite song coming on the radio at just the right time can seem to *confirm* a very recent decision, as reported by one of our study patients. "Right after my grandmother died, my boyfriend and I were driving home. Right when we got out of the car, 'our' (my and my grandmother's) song came on. I truly believe my grandmother was telling me that she really liked my boyfriend. That meant a lot because she knew that my parents were not very fond of him." The timely appearance of this song strengthened her belief in the relationship with her boyfriend. She was probably looking for a confirmation and might have found it elsewhere. Perhaps her parents were right, perhaps not. She took what she wanted from the death and the song.

Coincidences may also *challenge* someone's decision. A therapist friend told me this story. A forty-four-year-old woman was insisting to a friend that Donald Trump deserved to be re-elected as president. She "knew" that the Covid-19 virus was a hoax. Masks infringed on her freedom. As she was talking and repeatedly interrupting her friend's attempt to speak, she received a text message to call the nursing home where her mother was a resident. She was told that her mother had contracted Covid-19 and was seriously ill. The woman was terrified and embarrassed. She told her friend the news and began to question her support for Donald Trump.

In addition to aiding in decision making, coincidences offer many other useful possibilities.

Coincidences can *deliver what a person needs*. They can be arrows in Cupid's quiver. Across a crowded room a person might somehow know that that the sound of that stranger's laughter will echo again in the future. New friendships can be formed in the oddest ways. People may be reunited with lost loved ones and with lost pets through improbable coincidences. Needed help may appear through sudden coincidences, as rescuers from imminent danger or from the depths of despair. They may deliver a needed something—help, money, and things.

One of our research participants sent us this story. "Several years ago I was babysitting out in the country in a home that was very secluded. At lunch, I happened to open the blinds on the sliding glass door. At that very moment, I saw a man way out in a pasture on a tractor pulling a plow. In the instant that I glanced at him, the spring broke on the old tractor seat and the man fell off the seat and the back wheel of the tractor rolled over him, then his body got mangled under the blades of the plow as the tractor kept driving. If I hadn't opened those curtains at that very moment to see the man fall, he would be dead today. We were out in the middle of nowhere. The man later said nobody knew he was out in the pasture, and both of his lungs were punctured and rapidly filling with blood, so he couldn't yell for help. He couldn't walk because his legs were crushed and he was rapidly deteriorating. I called 911 and ran out to help him. Had I not seen him in that instant, he would've died."

Coincidences also provide *rewards for the curious*. Ideas swirl all around us, most profusely on the internet, which supplies high numbers of coincidences. Think of an idea and it appears on the screen, perhaps as part of an algorithm that tracks personal data. Other web coincidences follow less obvious programming. Information comes to us through other media—books, radio, TV, movies, and through other people. The serendipity super-encounterers find interesting, valuable information in all media forms and sometimes in the oddest places. But that's part of the fun and as well as being informative.

I was writing about human GPS and needed a biological basis for part of the explanation. At a loss, I turned away from writing to look at the online *New York Times*. In one of the headlines on the front page was "GPS." The story told how researchers had pinpointed "grid cells" near the hippocampus of rats that provide neural maps of places the rats had visited. Like the rats, we are constantly creating maps for our territories. The article provided a partial brain-based explanation for human GPS.[5]

Coincidences may also offer *aids for psychological change*. A sixty-five-year-old man was struggling with his long-standing "catastrophizing." If there was any possibility of something going wrong, he quickly went to the worst outcome and stayed there. His mind was occupied by a foreign army of imaginings of the most awful. In therapy with me, he admitted that he needed to keep the worrying going because he believed that his worry kept the bad things from happening. He was not praying to God but was praying to some unnamed angel that he thought required him to worry as a form of worship. In speaking this belief in the angel out loud, he more clearly saw its superstitious nature and questioned the practice.

A few days later, his daughter-in-law gave birth to her second child. The infant had a high bilirubin, which required their return to the hospital. He knew that the outcome was likely to be positive because when his daughter was born she too had a high bilirubin and was successfully treated by light therapy. He recognized that he did not need to worry because the angel was superstition and the outcome in the past was positive. The high bilirubin in his grandson became a serendipitous opportunity to practice what he had just learned.

Environmental events can often serve as empathic mirrors. The real-life dramas of others can mirror personal psychological problems and solutions. What one person does not like in someone else can reflect what that person doesn't like in himself or herself. The advice one person gives a friend could be the advice the adviser also needs to hear. What someone else just learned about oneself can also be a lesson for the listener. The movies, plays, and novels we see and read can mirror our current psychological problems and solutions.

Coincidences can serve as *aids to spiritual development*. We humans yearn to be part of something greater. In our hearts we know we are, but we may not know how to get there. Many methods have been devised to lift our minds out of the usual sensory reality into another sphere of experience. These methods include meditation in its many forms, psychedelics, fasting, group rituals, vision quests, near-death experiences, music, and yoga.

Coincidence awareness emerges through the apparently spontaneous appearance of meaningful coincidences in everyday life. Rather than removing people from the events of daily life as required by most spiritual practices, coincidence awareness immerses people more deeply into their current life and beyond. For some, meaningful coincidences become mini-mystical experiences. Reality as they know it melts into a brief fusion of mind and environment, bringing with it a numinous feeling of oneness with all there is. They might find themselves singing by a lake or a forest in the rain. As the rain slows, the sun peeps through, acting briefly like a spotlight on the not-so-solitary performance. They are on the stage of eternity.

Many grief-stricken people are surprised and comforted by the blooming of the favorite flower of the deceased in the winter. In her Ph.D. dissertation on synchronicity and grief, Jennifer Hill described how a gardenia bloomed in November after her grandfather died. That unexpected growth helped her grieving grandmother heal. Her grandmother knew very well that gardenia was his favorite flower.[6]

A friend of mine recounted the story of a grieving mother whose child had died at the age of five. Shortly after the funeral, at an outdoor brunch, a small bird landed on her breast and stayed there for some thirty minutes, looking around, chirping, and looking at her. The woman finally shooed the small bird away, and with that movement of her hand, she began to let go of her child.

These events bring human beings closer to the recognition that we participate in a much wider range of existence than conventional reality outlines for us.

Coincidences can provide clues *to extraordinary human abilities.* Psi capacities are well-documented in the history of religions[7] and their existence is supported by solid laboratory research,[8] which continues to be denied by conventional science. Anyone can deny data they do not want to believe or deny the implications of someone else's experience. But personal experiences, whether it's simulpathity or human GPS or precognition, make psi difficult to dismiss.

Finally, coincidences may be yet more commonplace than we realize. "Micro-serendipities" occur regularly in daily life without being recognized. Serendipity may constitute a more essential part of our life than we perhaps register in a world filled with so much planning, control, and presumed rationality. Encountering potentially interesting and useful things may play a crucial role in how we learn about the world.[9] One of my patients was befuddled about whether or not to proceed with a lawsuit against his former employer. For some reason he scrolled through a list of Irish folk wisdom and found these to be helpful. "Be careful of the anger of a patient person" and "Don't show your teeth until you are ready to bite." Some readers will find these saying useful. Are you one of them?

COINCIDENCE AS EXERCISE FOR THE MIND

Paying close attention to coincidences exercises the mind. Exercise benefits the mind just as it benefits the body.[10]

Coincidences inspire wonder and curiosity. Thinking about a coincidence is like peering into the unknown or trying to solve a riddle. "I wonder what this means." Wonder leads to curiosity, which drives solution seeking. Coincidences are like puzzles that lead people to think about their own identity and how relationships work. And they challenge our standard view about how reality works.

From the day we are born, curiosity becomes a driving force to explore unknown territories in search of answers and stimulation. Coincidences alert us to some of those mysteries. The solutions we come up with evoke feelings of pleasure. Dopamine squirts in the brain and boosts more curiosity adventures.

Curiosity helps humans to survive. The urge to explore and seek novelty enhances vigilance and adds to knowledge about our constantly changing environment.

Curious people are happier. Research has shown curiosity to be associated with higher levels of positive emotions, lower levels of anxiety, more satisfaction with life, and greater psychological well-being. It may be that people who are already happier are more curious.

Curiosity boosts achievement. Studies reveal that curiosity leads to more enjoyment and participation in school and higher academic achievement, as well as greater learning, engagement, and performance at work.

Curiosity expands empathy by pointing attention to the minds of others. By limiting personal projections and maintaining neutrality, one can travel into the mind of the other person, riding curiosity's beam of energized attention.[11]

But curiosity also has its downsides. The saying "curiosity killed the cat" warns against unnecessary investigation and experimentation. The cat went someplace he should not have gone. Going down a dark alley just to see what's there can be dangerous. Delving too deeply into the private life of others can reveal facts that might be better left hidden. Curiosity may be driven by a deep-seated discomfort with uncertainty and the need to come up with any solution that quiets this discomfort.

Too much curiosity about coincidences can become an obsession and detract from living life. Coincidences can become like clickbait, coaxing people down rabbit holes of confusion and irrelevance.

Coincidences strengthen the self-observer. Most human beings are capable of observing their own thinking and feelings. They can think about the events in their minds. The self-observer is the mind's organ of self-awareness.[12] It can scan the personal past, the present, and future. The self-observer can connect emotions, intuition, thoughts, and images to events in the environment, including ideas about events in the minds of other people. Self-observation includes meta-cognition, which focuses primarily on thoughts.

The self-observer can be strengthened in several ways. Keeping a diary gives the mind distance from its own activities. Writing down one's thoughts and feelings enables the person to view themselves more objectively. Meditation is another tool that can provide "distance" between the workings of the mind and the ability to observe them. Mindfulness meditation counsels meditators to let thoughts go without judgment and bring attention back to the breath. This practice pulls awareness increasingly further away from the thoughts and feelings themselves. And under the right conditions mind-expanding substances like psychedelics can provide a heightened perspective on one's mind as well as reality itself.

Sometimes outside help is needed to encourage the use of the self-observer. Psychotherapy requires active collaboration between the self-observers of both patient and therapist. Patients are asked to "step back" to objectively report mental-emotional activity. The therapist attempts to scan the activities of the patient's mind through the portal of the patient's self-observer reports. Therapists also scan their own thought-image-emotion activity for clues about what might be useful to say in helping patients change. Together the pair create an alliance between the two self-observers—the self-observer alliance.

To notice a coincidence involves simultaneously holding in mind two or more separate events. As they are being held in awareness, the self-observer can examine the various meanings of the paired events, including their similarity, probability, emotional charge, personal significance, and possible explanation.

Like a physical exercise regimen, coincidence awareness can make major demands on the self-observer and strengthen its capacity to operate. But thinking about inner states and events can be overdone. It can paralyze one's ability to act by burying awareness in *what if, could be,* and *regret.* Thoughts and emotions can spin through the mind with no resolution. Similarly, a tantalizing coincidence seemingly ripe with meaning can draw the self-observer into a muddy quagmire.

But as people become more familiar with their own self-observers, they may find themselves operating with a second self-observer. The second self-observer observes the range and details of the activities of the first self-observer. Getting out of a mental quagmire can be assisted by activating the second self-observer. From its heightened perspective, the second self-observer gains leverage to stop the endless spiraling. Hints for how to activate and use this second self-observer come from examining the self-observer alliance established when one person tunes into the activity of another person's self-observer. The outside observer follows the details of the primary person's first observer. Therapists generally perform this second self-observer function for their patients. The patient may then identify with the therapist's observer to help conceptualize and shape their own second observer. This same strengthening of second self-observer can take place between any two people who carefully listen to each other.

An acquaintance of mine at our ecstatic dance gathering described how his basic thought programming inhibited him from acting on his intuition. In considering whether he should come up to me and engage in conversation, he heard his first self-observer activate the usual command, saying, "Don't do, it will turn out bad." Noticing this response, his second self-observer activated a contrary command: "Follow this impulse and see what happens." We had a great conversation.

Coincidences expand intuition. The often-opaque meanings of coincidences can push rational analysis to its limits and therefore require another source of information. Intuition is knowing that you know without knowing how, that is without direct evidence or rational analysis.

For those who rely primarily on rationality, information coming to awareness without an obvious source can be troubling. Yet, people often know many things without knowing how they know them. With practice, letting this "illogical" information into awareness can complement and supersede rationally produced information. A gut feeling or an emotional urge or a still small voice can present useful interpretations of a coincidence. The process of learning to trust intuitive messages requires rational testing of the qualities of various intuitive inputs to identify the channels that are consistently helpful.

Testing out intuitive channels parallels our probes of the trustworthiness of the external world. A new acquaintance seems trustworthy. How might she harm me? Is she consistent? Does she do what she says she will do? How might she help me?

Intuitive messages can be tested in a similar way. Which ones should be avoided? Which ones regularly produce desired outcomes? Which ones trigger caution? Repeated testing will clarify those automatic responses to use, which ones to question, and which ones to discard.

Using a coincidence may mean acting on an intuitive message. Without quick action, the pairing of similar events may not ripen into a useful meaningful coincidence. When Jung heard tapping on the window of his consulting room, he followed his intuition. He got up, opened the window, and brought into the room a scarab-like beetle, after his highly rational patient had just told him of her dream about a scarab. The synchronicity is the event that startled her into therapeutic change.

By taking the wrong elevator a journalism student accidentally ended up in the living room of the employer he was seeking. Surprised by the situation created by this unintentional trespassing, he fled, instead of seizing the moment. Life presents possibilities. Quick action makes some of them real. The courage to act grows out of an increasingly refined intuition. Refinement comes with practice, with mistakes. The journalism student had not developed enough confidence in his intuition to act on what he needed.

For those who rely primarily on intuition, rationality may seem cumbersome and unnecessary. The answers come effortlessly. No need to laboriously analyze. However, without the effective guidance of good reasoning about the limits of intuition and the constraints of reality, intuition may lead to problematic interpretations of coincidences.

Coincidences sharpen rationality. Rationality aids probability estimates and reinforces the fact that the coincider is one of many people having similar experiences and that its personal usefulness may have several possibilities. Wishful thinking arising from intuition can be counter-balanced by knowing what is most likely rather than what is most desired. Meeting a stranger unexpectedly connected to a desired job may trigger the feeling that the job is meant to be. The feeling may require a rational assessment of real-world limitations and potentials. Attempts to understand coincidences sharpens both intuition and rationality and ideally leads to a practical balance between the two.

Coincidences can help people to inhibit their premature labeling of feelings and judgments. Some coincidences deserve patience to be understood. In the desire to grasp its meaning, the coincider may declare this coincidence to signal something wonderful (like a new romance, friendship, discovery, invention, job, a step in spiritual development, or evidence of an extraordinary ability). Labeling it as wonderful (or terrible) can restrict its unfolding. The coincidence could lead to a very short-term positive that devolves into something awful. Disappointment and anger would follow. The meanings may become clearer after a good night's sleep, a discussion with someone, and time.

Coincidences exercise the skill for turning neutral experiences into positive ones. Imagine installing in the mind or brain a little app that turns the perception of neutral or mildly negative events into positive events. Many life events may make a person feel anxiety, anger, disappointment, regret, or sadness. But the attribution of positive or negative feelings toward an event is often a matter of choice. Take for example, romantic coincidences, which can sometimes seem like promises about the future. The feeling of *wow* with someone can lead that person to feel like the couple's future is rosy for eternity. And then, after a short or long time, reality bites; the relationship ends. Was the relationship positive or negative? The individuals can either be bitterly disappointed in how the fates have toyed with their future or be grateful for the great feelings they've experienced and what was learned from their time together.

Here's the surprise. The app has already been installed in each mind-brain. Coincidence outcomes can be molded to a best fit, not necessarily keeping with the initial unfolding. These phrases propel the imaginary app: "Turn stumbling blocks into stepping stones." "The only failure is to fail to learn from failure." "Look for what you can learn from this." With practice the app for turning the mind toward the positive can become increasingly more agile and effective.

Meaningful coincidences mimic interpersonal role induction. Human speech carries both a message (the digital, word-based communication) and a nonverbal request (the analog, visual-behavioral-emotional communication). The nonverbal includes efforts to induce the listener to assume a role desired by the speaker. The role request hides in plain sight. The role request is usually not consciously evident to the speaker who is caught up in saying the words, or to the listener who is trying to understand what is being said. This is subconscious role induction.[13,14]

Coincidences, too, may communicate both a direct message and induce a role response in the coincider. The simultaneous experience of choking between my father and me told me that simulpathity is real. Coupled with the fact that he died on my birthday, the coincidence induced me to write about him, repeatedly. As if he were saying, "Remember me!" Through telling this story, I am honoring him.

Noticing how coincidences can induce responses in the coincider exercises the conscious ability to notice subconscious role induction from oneself and from others.

Coincidences exercise the skill for thinking simultaneously of polarity and continuum thinking. Most people seem to prefer to think in either a polarity or a continuum. Less mental effort is required when using a standard information filter. Holding in mind the polarity *and* the continuum at the same time stretches the mind.

Individuals, to varying degrees, participate in creating coincidences. Because human responsibility for coincidences varies, explanations for coincidences lie on a continuum of human responsibility between God or the Universe and random chance. Many people prefer either probability or God and have difficulty accepting the variable contributions of the coincider himself or herself. Realistic understanding of coincidences relies on incorporating the poles and the continuum since probability and the unknown also contribute to varying degrees. Sometimes the unknown final cause of God (or the Universe or consciousness) becomes the best explanation. Sometimes probability or random chance are the best explanations, and sometimes the individual has created the coincidence. More often all three contribute to explanations. Each coincidence has a probability of happening. Many coincidences cannot be fully explained by the coincider's thoughts and actions. Some mystery remains that may be answered by one or several of the theories described earlier. To conceptualize coincidences and other aspects of reality as both polarities and continuums exercises the mind.

In addition to possible explanations, coincidences exercise polarity-continuum thinking in at least three other ways.

1. We tend to believe that each mind is totally separate from what is outside the mind, that the skull separates the inner world from the outside world. Mind-environment polarity is much engrained in a lot of human thinking. Yet coincidences show us that minds are also embedded in their contexts. The mind is stretched by contemplating both the polarity of what's inside the mind versus what's outside the mind, while also considering each pole as part of a continuum that, to varying degrees, connects individual minds with the environment.

2. The unique-same polarity can also be seen as a continuum. Some people prefer to think that everyone is different. Some people prefer to see how everyone is the same. People are both the same and unique. Like coincidences, they vary in the degrees of their uniqueness.

3. The skeptic and the believer are another polarity pair, which may be regarded as the debunking pseudo-skeptic and true believer. The degree of willingness to question beliefs and openness to evidence form the continuum.

As you've read in this book, coincidences can be very useful to individuals, groups, organizations, and humanity. They not only exercise individual minds, but also help us to navigate and learn about reality. To build upon what we have learned, I am leading the creation and development of The Coincidence Project, which you can read about in appendix 1. I hope you'll join us in sharing your stories of meaningful coincidences, serendipity, and synchronicity. For more information, you can also check out my podcast on Spreaker, YouTube at youtube.com/c/Coinciders /videos, or on my website coincider.com. As we connect and learn about the evolution of human self-awareness, both individually and collectively, I hope we will come to more deeply understand our world and use coincidences to help heal our collective selves.

The Collective Human Organism

Throughout human history, coincidences have served as clues to undiscovered aspects of the natural world, individual minds, interpersonal relationships, spiritual evolution, science, technology, art, business, and society. Their surprise stimulates curiosity, which activates personal self-observers. Because many meaningful coincidences involve striking parallels between mind events and environmental events, examination of their uses and explanations can expand human understanding of our relationships between mind and environment. Mind-mind and some mind-object (where the object is a person) coincidences point to close connections between and among people. These close connections suggest that each human being may be part of something greater. Common phrases suggesting this reality include "we're all in this together" or "everything is connected." The something greater can be conceptualized as the Collective Human Organism (CHO), with each person functioning as a cell in this organism. This idea begins to answer the question about how each of us is part of the greater whole. Meaningful coincidences illuminate the invisible threads that connect us to each other, to our environment, and to the other living creatures surrounding us. They highlight our shared mental and emotional participation in the psychosphere. They also help to pave the way to crystalizing the unique gift each person brings to their participation in the CHO by sharpening their own identity while simultaneous illuminating their connecting invisible currents. The CHO may be imagined in human form to stride our planet with its head in the clouds, its mind connected to its Higher Self in the psychosphere, its feet moving through the earth. Currently those big feet are stomping out the life of many living things and those big hands are selfishly grabbing resources with little regard for its habitat.

Today, there is more and more frequent reference to Earth, to the planet, and to the totality of our habitat. So much so, in fact, that now the idea of Earth as an evolving, giant organism is part of ordinary conversation. The CHO idea will take time to take its place in everyday conversations. The very popular history of humanity, the book *Sapiens,*[1] has helped to propel the idea that we human beings are also an evolving organism.

Several conclusions follow, the first being that the CHO has a mind. This mind would have a collective conscious and collective unconscious. The collective conscious holds current social, cultural, scientific, religious, and media-generated ideas. The collective unconscious holds memories, conflicts, emotions, and the multiple selves of diverse human self-identities.

Like individuals, the CHO also could develop a collective self-observer. Using patterns suggested by systematic analysis of large numbers of coincidence stories, the collective self-observer could look for new clues that help to peer behind the curtain of our ignorance about how to proceed. Particular emphasis would be placed on clues that will help to heal the CHO and divert it from destroying our habitat. These serendipity- and synchronicity-fueled discoveries will supplement rational, logical approaches to investigating reality and solving the multiple threats to human existence.

To survive, the CHO would need to become more aware of itself and the destruction it is causing and to develop a collective conscience to guide its ethical and moral development. As a cell in the CHO, each person has something to contribute to its overall successful functioning. Each person is encouraged to ask, "What can I contribute to the best functioning of the Collective Human Organism?" Personal coincidences will help to answer this question. We are in a battle for people's imagination about the future. Can we gather together to first imagine and then acknowledge the existence of our Collective Human Organism?

CHALLENGES TO THE COLLECTIVE HUMAN ORGANISM

The CHO is tortured by autoimmune diseases like war, poverty, starvation, police brutality, religious hatred, autocratic governments, corporate amorality, and institutionalized racism. The body is attacking itself. It is also afflicted by blood clots closing off arteries to large groups of cells through callous indifference to mass migration, poverty, starvation, immigrants, inadequate healthcare, inadequate public health, mental illness, and drug abuse. The deliberate actions and inaction by governments, corporations, and the very wealthy are depriving large groups of cells of nutrition.

Like most individuals, the CHO has several competing selves. One kind of self is certain it will survive anything because their God or their money or both will save them, that Mother Earth is here to serve them, and that her bounty is endless. Another kind of self is convinced that total annihilation is imminent, that Mother Earth is being stretched to the limit of her gift-giving ability. Still another recognizes the wisdom of including the consciousness of animals, plants, and fungi in imaging the future. These selves are barely acknowledged by the other selves because each one is striving for domination of the mind of the CHO. They are battling for the organism's images of the future. The multiple conflicting forces are creating chaos in the collective mind. These forces need recognition and organizing to bring the coherence necessary for imagining a livable future.

The development of the necessary collective mind is underway.

The internet is providing an increasingly strong scaffolding for the operations of the psychosphere. Our minds are increasingly tethered to it as a metaphor to our connections within the psychosphere. Covid-19 has threatened human beings worldwide to embrace or reject in unison scientifically advised behaviors. These two groups share similar thought patterns. Like many coincidences, the virus mirrors the mind of the CHO. The virus destroys its hosts in order to replicate. Humans are destroying their planetary host while endlessly replicating. Earth is trying to tell us we are not masters; we are guests. Global warming is issuing another challenge and solidifying the cohesion of polarizing groups. Meaningful coincidence abound in our environment. Look at these two words *environmental* and *mental*. *Mental* is contained within the word *environmental*. As they have been for humankind for all of our existence on Earth, coincidences can provide meaningful clues for adaptation to our evolving environment. We have to look.

As we look, we will need to fully recognize that life on Earth is filled with polarities. Coincidences will help connect polarities to the continuum of which they are a part.

The Coincidence Project, which is founded on the principle that coincidences can offer clues to how reality works, can participate in this effort as those clues can be applied to discovering practical methods for correcting the course of the CHO and its individual cells with their connections to the whole.

DEVELOPING THE COLLECTIVE SELF-OBSERVER

Humankind can develop its self-observer through the coalescence of highly developed individual self-observers. As mentioned earlier the examination of meaningful coincidences exercises the personal self-observer and can also aid that process for the CHO. Through the use of the collective self-observer, humanity can develop a collective vision for the future of Earth and the necessary collective conscience. The process begins with recognizing the problem. Just as an alcoholic needs to declare, "My name is Adam. I am an alcoholic," our CHO needs to first declare that there is a problem. "My name is Humankind. I am addicted to constant material growth. I want more psychological, interpersonal, and social growth."

A large swath of humanity cannot, does not, or is afraid to observe their own minds. Some are too preoccupied with the challenges of survival or caught up in the demands of constant busyness. Others could activate their self-observers but refuse. They do not want to look at their own motivations because they might see something they would have to change, which takes effort. So they adopt views of themselves that do not require self-examination. "I am just fine the way I am." "My problems are caused by other people. I am a victim." "Other people's problems are not my problems." "I am responsible for only myself and my family."

Many people hold so firmly to beliefs that evidence is not capable of softening them. The firmness seems to be generated by intense emotions supported by different lines of intentions. Some hold tightly to a specific religious belief, which promises them that if you believe this way, you and your loved ones will have life everlasting. That's a strong inducement to believe with complete devotion, where no questioning or doubt is allowed without calling into question that promise of an eternal reward. Related, and also separate sometimes, is that sharing a fervent belief with others provides solid insurance to continue being accepted as part of the group. The desire for group membership runs deep in the human psyche. Self-reflection on each of these beliefs threatens the possibility of eternal life and group membership. The tight boundaries surrounding fundamentalist religions may not be flexible enough for loosening. Similarly those who believe their wealth will save them from the ravages of global warming will also strongly resist loosening of their entitled boundaries. Some earthbound polarities will not adjust to the evident threats.

On the other hand there are highly spiritual people who believe "it is all good" that "things are as they should be." No! This attitude is a form of spiritual bypassing in which the person continues self-elevation to spiritual realms in the belief that their higher energy level will induce others into the same state. Unfortunately, like many dramatic psychedelic experiences, the feeling dissipates in regular life unless it is somehow nurtured. Spiritual elevation needs to be accompanied by learning how to love others and to be loved by others. These are not easy things to do. Bypassing the inevitable conflicts emerging from people in groups through spiritual lovingkindness avoids the hard interpersonal work.

The height of maladaptive thinking is repeating the same thing and expecting a different outcome. What other futures are there? Throughout human history one theme has endured—apocalypse. This future theme has been enshrined in the Western mind through Revelations, the last book in the Christian Bible. The world is destroyed and only the true believers are saved. As philosopher Michael Grosso points out,[2] other cultures preceded John of Patmos (not John the Baptist) in predicting total destruction. Only those who hold certain beliefs, or belong to certain groups, or who have distinguishing physical qualities, will survive. Science fiction often hammers the same dystopian theme. It's much easier to imagine annihilation and its variations than a complex, evolving, compassionate, and loving future in which the cells of the CHO strive to heal each other through love and conflict resolution. In brain terms this conflict mirrors the generally opposite functions of the amygdala and the nucleus accumbens. The amygdala is the seat of anxiety, which channels anger. The nucleus accumbens releases dopamine, a key feel-good neurochemical. Rage vs love is one of the fundamental choices of the CHO. This includes finding a balance between the two, a continuum for the polarity.

The self-fulfilling prophecy has a respected history in psychology. If you believe you will be rejected by others, you will subconsciously behave in ways that will "prove" your belief. If you believe that the world will be destroyed, that increases the likelihood that the world will be destroyed because you will subconsciously act in ways that promote the anticipated destruction. If you hold a clear vision of a beneficial future, you will behave in ways that increase the likelihood of a beneficial future. It is not enough to passively hope it all works out. You must also act! If you don't imagine where you are going, you will go where other people take you.

Some people will not recognize their potential functioning in the CHO. Will they be like skin cells sloughing off to feed the Earth? Perhaps guidance from coincidences will assist those who are too blind to see the threats and threads that can unite us all.

Our CHO can imagine a future for Earth and its inhabitants. But will it? Do we have the will to do it?

Living beings have two major survival modes: fight or cooperate. Wolves cooperate to eat other animals. Fungi and trees nurture each other. Human groups can cooperate or kill one another. What will the mind of the CHO choose? Our vision for the future will shape the major decisions in the ever present now. An ethical collective consciousness can empower us to imagine, individually and collectively, and then to create not only sustainable future but also a fun-filled future for humankind and all life on Earth. The groundwork is being laid for Playground Earth and for Earth University, where we can dance at the learning-entertainment interface. I imagine that astute interpretations of our many collective synchronicities and serendipities will guide this transformation from the many antagonistic polarities among human groups into conflicts from which we can evolve spiritually and interpersonally.

Acknowledgments

Patrick Huyghe edited a partially organized jumble of ideas into a streamlined manuscript. Always supportive and kind and always a very good friend.

Juliet Trail has long been a steadfast friend, supporter, and teacher, helping to strengthen both the foundation of this book and the foundation of The Coincidence Project

Leaders and members of the division of perceptual studies at the University of Virginia provided an exquisite sounding board for my updates on this project. I met Patrick through those meetings as well as Frank Pasciuti and Michael Grosso with whom stimulating conversations helped develop this book.

Dancers of the Charlottesville Dance cooperative and leaders of the 5Rhythm dance classes inspired me through the profoundly beautiful experiences they had created and maintained. The dancers themselves were seekers like me with whom I could learn and expand mutually intriguing ideas. Ken Laster and Ann Kite were particularly instructive.

Barbara Groves, my therapist colleague and dear friend, energized me with her deeply supportive emotions and our lively discussions about psychological and spiritual matters.

Russ Federman connected me to *Psychology Today* where I was able to blog coincidence ideas to a large and receptive audience. Ideas from some of those blog posts were incorporated into this book.

High school friend and author Dave Morris contributed intermittent wry commentary. He is always insightful and challenging.

Thanks also to Martin Plimmer and Brian King and to a few other collectors of coincidence stories: my son Karlen Beitman with your reluctant reports of coincidences, Walter Beitman and Dennis Beitman, Madeleine Laurent, Gina Jamrozy, Julia Spencer, Gail O'Connell, and Larry Dossey.

I am deeply grateful to Carl Jung and to Horace Walpole. Jung's pioneering and courageous introduction of synchronicity to the Western mind planted the seed from which this book has grown. Walpole, preceding and unrecognized by Jung, planted the seed of meaningful coincidence with his concept of serendipity.

And to my grandchildren, Zoe, Max, and Rose—I hope one day you get a sense for what your Zayde was doing. Aaron, my son, and Liza, my daughter-in-law, thank-you for the love you have brought into my life. And Boomer, for your healthy and supportive skepticism

Thank you Richard Grossinger of Sacred Planet for seeing the promise is this manuscript. Project editor Kayla Toher of Inner Traditions and copy editor Sarah Galbraith lovingly embraced my ideas. . . . Thank you for making them more real!

Gibbs Williams connected me with XZBN radio, which enabled me to conduct 138 interviews with more than 100 people dedicated to studying coincidences, and then I was able to interview 80 more people (and still counting) on the *Connecting with Coincidence* podcast 2.0. Those interviewees, including psychologists, business consultants, academic leaders, shamans, teachers, and musicians, deepened and broadened my understanding of coincidences. My thanks to: Tito Abao, Eben Alexander, Marcus Anthony, Thomas Baruzzi, Patrick Belisle,

Rosalyn Berne, Anna Heleen Bijl, Lennart Björneborn, Ralph Blumenthal, Gary Bobroff, Carol Bowman, Alexis Brooks, Laurence Browne, Larry Burk, Christian Busch, Lisa Bucksbaum, Bethany Butzer, Joseph (Joe) Cambray, Étzel Cardeña, Jim Carpenter, Cynthia Cavalli, Deepak Chopra, Christine Clawley, Mike Clelland, Suzanne Clores, Samantha Copeland, Pam Coronado, JD (Julie) Cross, John D'Earth, Brian Dailey, Jason DeBord, Sherrie Dillard, Doug Dillon, Larry Dossey, Brendan Engen, Sanda Erdelez, Pippa Erlich, Sally Rhine Feather, Frankie Fihn, Kiana Fitzgerald, Ken Godevenos, Ray Grasse, Richard Grossinger, Michael Grosso, Wendy Halley, Charles Hamner, David Hand, Buddy Helm, David Hench, Rey Hernandez, Eric Hill, Robert Hopcke, John Ironmonger, Audrey Irvine, Tara MacIsaac, Sky Nelson-Isaacs, Michael Jawer, Joseph Jaworski, Dahamindra Jeevan, Linnea Johansson (Star), Frank Joseph, Amelía Aeon Karris, Ritu Kaushal, Gordon Keirle-Smith, Edward F. Kelly, Michelle Kempton, Pagan Kennedy, Neil Killion, Jeffrey Kripal, John Kruth, Noah Lampert, Josh Lane, Mary Kay Landon, Tobias Raayoni Last, Laura Lee, Joshua Lengfelder, Ralph Lewis, Lumari, Trish Macgregor, Chris Mackey, Roderick Main, Christa Mariah, Julie Mariel, Terry Marks-Tarlow, Helen Marlo, Joe Mazur, Robert (Rob) McConnell, Bonnie Mceneaney Mcnamara, Alessandra Melas, Philip Merry, Greg Meyerhoff, Kathy Meyers, Jeffrey Mishlove, Julia Mossbridge, Karen Newell, Magda Osman, Jennifer Palmer, Robert (Bob) Pargament, Frank Pasciuti, Janet Payne, Marieta Pehlivanova, Robert Perry, Jessica Pryce-Jones, Dean Radin, Sharon Hewitt Rawlette, Peter Richards, Wendy Ross, Harley Rotbart, Nora Ruebrook, Pninit Russo-Netzer, Martin Sand, Sabrina Sauer, Kia Scherr, Gary Schwartz, Rupert Sheldrake, Yanik Silver, Terje Simonsen, David Spiegelhalter, Maureen St. Germain, Sophie Strand, Morgan Stebbins, David Strabala, Richard Tarnas, Yvonne Smith Tarnas, Scott Taylor, Denise Thompson, John Townley, Juliet Trail, Jim Tucker, Diogo Valadas Ponte, James Clement Van Pelt, Saskia Von Diest, Mustafa Wahid, Ros Watt, Andrew Weil, Barbara Harris Whitfield, Gibbs Williams, James Williford, Gary Wimmer, Katrin (Kat) Windsor, Peter Woodbury, and Matthew Zylstra.

APPENDIX I

The Coincidence Project

Despite concerns that coincidences are rare, or signs of a psychiatric disorder, research has shown that meaningful coincidences commonly occur.[1,2,3,4] The Coincidence Project desires to inspire a leap forward in the evolution of human self-awareness individually, interpersonally, and collectively in order to develop novel problem-solving ideas to limit human planetary threats and tilt our trajectory toward love and fun. The keys to transformation of human consciousness include knowing, as Nat King Cole sang, that "the greatest thing you'll ever learn / Is just to love and be loved in return."

The Coincidence Project was created to help people recognize the interconnectedness of all life through appreciating and sharing coincidence experiences. The vision is to illuminate the invisible currents that connect and unify us.

Our mission is to educate the public about meaningful coincidences and encourage you to share your stories of meaningful coincidences, serendipity, and synchronicity in order to inspire the leap forward in the evolution of human self-awareness, individually, interpersonally, and collectively. The project will accomplish this mission by:

> enhancing interpersonal and ecological compassion through connections discovered in world-wide coincidence storytelling and the understanding to be found in them by sharing with others;

promoting people, called coincidence ambassadors, who are passion-
ate about representing meaningful coincidences;

educating people about the wide-ranging helpfulness of synchronicity and serendipity in human experience;

creating the coincidence research group to study patterns in coincidence stories;

defining an ethics of coincidence functions;

gathering global experts to expand collective understanding of
meaningful coincidences; and

relying on synchronicity and serendipity to guide and accelerate the
progress of these missions.

Please feel free to add our mission statement to websites and social
media as enticement to bring people to The Coincidence Project's website. Achieving our mission is a three-pronged effort: to encourage global
coincidence dialogues and collections, to promote research efforts based
on cases collected, and to establish coincidence studies as an academic
discipline. We plan to accomplish this mission through finding and
developing committed researchers and by hosting retreats, seminars, and
discussion groups for the general public both online and in person.

COINCIDENCE DIALOGUES

The first part of The Coincidence Project is essentially a coincidence
story collection effort. People experiencing coincidences, either personal
or professional, will be urged to record their stories and to tell others
about them. Our motto is: "After you talk about the weather, tell a
coincidence story." When one person tells a coincidence story to another,
the listener may be reminded of a personal example that then can be told
in return. Telling coincidence stories to each other generates interpersonal
connections through their heightened shared emotion. These interchanges
can also expand personal acceptance of our shared group mind.

People will be encouraged to record personal stories in their own

Diary of a Coincider. We can help people speak about and write up their coincidence stories, encouraging them to keep in mind that most of the time their coincidence story is much more compelling to them than it is to others. (See appendix 2: "How to Write and Tell Coincidence Stories.")

Synchronicity soirees can be promoted. These small group gatherings in homes, in community centers, and through online meetings aim to create an arena in which to safely and deeply explore the minds and emotions of others through coincidence storytelling. Video-conferencing story telling can be recorded for analysis. Existing coincidence-based social media networks will be asked to share their stories with the Project. We have launched a monthly call, the Coincidence Café, to provide a virtual gathering place in which you can have some synchroniciTea and some serendipiTea while exploring rotating topics and small group discussion prompts.

Coincidence chat rooms like the Café can be yet another source of stories to be shared as well as social media sites like Clubhouse where Coincidence Ambassadors gather with anyone who wants to participate. Those coinciders who offer multiple stories with the same theme will be urged to join interest groups of similar coincider types to explore their particular observations on coincidences.

Other methods for facilitating coincidence dialogues involve recording coincidence use in classrooms, businesses, narratives (movies, novels, history), and in nature; writing coincidence story books for children; writing and singing coincidence songs; creating synchronicity and serendipity video games; tracking meaningful coincidences in the metaverse; and hosting larger gatherings, including film festivals, in which the audience is charged with recognizing coincidences.

THE COINCIDENCE AMBASSADORS

With the assistance of Juliet Trail, I have organized a body of active coincidence ambassadors from across the spectrum of interested professions to carry out the missions of The Coincidence Project. We have also identified a group of other supporting experts, the coincidence allies, to support the work of the ambassadors. These transdisciplinary coincident agents include representatives from physics, Jungian psychology serendipity research, parapsychology, psychiatry, psychology, neuropsychology, psychotherapy and counseling, humanistic nonprofits, the narrative arts and visual arts, organizational consulting, spiritual traditions, contemplative arts, shamanism, theology, philosophy, social media technology, and other students of coincidences.

THE COINCIDENCE RESEARCH GROUP

The coincidence research group will be the research arm of The Coincidence Project. It will collect coincidence stories from global coincidence dialogues in a systematic way. These can be written out, recorded in an audio file, or videotaped. The stories can be fed into an artificial intelligence algorithm to uncover potentially useful clues as to their origin. They can become entries in big data analytics. The development of the system can be guided by serendipity as well as programming logic. This effort will serve as the leading edge for new initiatives to advance research into understanding and ethically using coincidences. Ultimately it will search for clues to how reality works to sharpen methods for the spiritual and psychological evolution of individuals, their interpersonal relationships, and their social groups.

Coincidence-friendly software engineers will be recruited to help develop content analytic methods to judge the likelihood that a coincidence is either a source of new information or expands knowledge about how they may be used. The research group will use the information gathered to develop a cartography of Earth's mental atmosphere, the psychosphere.

The research group is asking: What are the conditions that seem to increase coincidences? Coincidences are created through an interaction between people and their environment. What powers this interaction into generating coincidences?

Through this work, high frequency coinciders will be identified.

Then, to go deeper, we will ask: What more can we learn about their characteristics? We will be clarifying more fully what makes these coinciders so sensitive, what they do to create their coincidences, and how they interpret and use them.

The collection of stories will identify people whose coincidences suggest that they might possess extraordinary abilities like telepathy, clairvoyance, human GPS, and precognition. The research group will develop ways to help them manifest these abilities, within ethical guidelines, of course.

The context in which coincidences seem to increase will also be evaluated. Life stressors need more systematic attention since they have so regularly been reported to be correlated with an increase in coincidence frequency. The association of grief and coincidence, as mentioned previously, was the subject of a doctoral dissertation.[5] Other conditions to be studied include sickness, romance, and job stressors with normal life comparators.

Physical settings also require evaluation. Individual, couple, and family psychotherapy provide potentially controllable settings to study the likely regular occurrence of coincidences. Therapy provides fertile ground for coincidence creation and detection because therapy increases emotional intensity, opens all participants to the contents of their own and other minds, and increases mind-context intersections. How can this potentially vibrant cache of meaningful coincidences be mined?

The research group can test the hypothesis that coincidences occur regularly but are often missed because of the absence of a heightened emotional state or sufficient attention. To study this question, the project will define a specific time and place for ongoing reports. A baseline study will examine coincidence type and frequency in a circumscribed everyday situation like a supermarket. A comparison group could be a high-energy gathering like a music festival or coincidence conference. Not only would standardized questions accompany the subjects when a coincidence is noted, but real-time video cameras, GPS locators, and subsequent interviews would also be employed. This study would apply current anthropological methods for gathering data and then apply computer programs to define patterns of coincidence that might not be readily discerned by the human mind alone.

The research group will establish an infrastructure for coincidence counseling referrals, for those overwhelmed by coincidences. With permission, coincidence counseling stories will be entered into the ongoing story collection database.

COINCIDENCE STUDIES

The coincidence research group will seek to establish the study of coincidences as an academic discipline. This effort could include creating a peer reviewed *Journal of Coincidence Studies* and a popular magazine tentatively titled *Coincidences Today*.

To establish the field of coincidence studies, an interest in coincidences must garner the energetic attention of sufficiently large numbers of people positioned to help it develop. An enthusiastic general public will motivate popular media discussions on the subject. Public and popular media interest, and works such as this one, will then drive the idea into the academic and grant-funding arenas. Research results and accompanying academic interest will add to growing support, leading to the establishment of formal interdisciplinary units in and outside of academics to promote the use and study of coincidences.

The Yale SynchroSummit, held in October 2010, marked the first focused gathering for the study of meaningful coincidences that included the full spectrum of competing theories. Presenters discussed definitions of synchronicity, the value of studying synchronicity, its basic patterns and explanations, and its challenges to mainstream science.[6] More such summits would help to accelerate the field's development.

The first meeting of the Serendipity Society was held in September 2019 in London. The Serendipity Society nurtures an active network of serendipity researchers, promotes rigorous interdisciplinary research, and works toward the reciprocal relationship between research and theory development. The Serendipity Society is a viable and growing group of enthusiastic investigators with a promising future of rich contributions to the study of coincidences.

The inaugural Coincidence Ambassador meeting of The Coincidence Project was held virtually in October 2020. The attendees included coincidence book authors, business consultants, a synchronicity filmmaker, a shaman, a creator of a synchronicity card deck, a philosopher, a neuropsychologist, a counselor, a compassion-meditation teacher, and a researcher of serendipity super-encounterers. I was gratified to see that the participants shared very similar ways of thinking about coincidences. Despite their strongly different professional contexts, coincidence experiences created similar ways of thinking about them. This first meeting suggested that coincidence studies can easily become interdisciplinary, because this work starts with many shared assumptions based on common experiences. As of February 2022, these coincidence ambassadors have met seventeen times, forming a cohesive group who are preparing to launch a multipronged effort to encourage coincidence storytelling, reporting, and research.

Coincidences will serve as guiding influences in the development of a coincidence studies program. Our organizational mind will be alert to those unexpected, unpredictable correlations that can richly populate everyday life. The relevant coincidences can be presented to our consultants for interpretation and possible guidance. The incorporation of meaningful coincidences into a living, growing organization will help keep us flexible, open, and studying in real time just what we might be studying in other systematic ways. This process may produce principles that are applicable to other organizations.

A major challenge in the development of this new discipline is providing a systematic place for subjectivity and consciousness. Meaningful coincidences are fully dependent upon the mind of the observer. Without subjective recognition most coincidences do not exist. Science has yet to develop a methodology and an accompanying language that includes the subjective. The study of coincidences will join other efforts to make the subjective part of future scientific dialogues. I hope you'll join us on The Coincidence Project's website to follow our progress.

QUESTIONS FOR REFLECTION

The following questions are provided to help you reflect on this book. If you're part of a book club, be sure to discuss similarities and differences among group members. If you're interested in joining a group to discuss coincidences, check out The Coincidence Project's website.

- Which specific passages struck you as significant—interesting, profound, amusing, illuminating, surprising, disturbing, sad . . . ?
- What did you learn generally? What was your biggest takeaway specifically?
- How do you score on the weird coincidence survey? (Go to coincider.com and then click "Your Coincidences.")
- Think of a personal coincidence story. Which category does it fit into? (p. 22)
- Describe how a coincidence influenced an important decision.
- What kind of coincider are you? Which theories are most compatible with your thinking? (p. 93)
- What is your fundamental belief about the nature of reality? Did you view about personal responsibility shift after reading this book? How so?
- How do you react to the idea of meta-coincidences? (p. 46)
- What does the phrase *Luck is when opportunity meets preparation* mean to you? What does persistence have to do with serendipity? (p. 75)
- Which examples struck you in the section on problematic coincidences? (p. 82)
- How has your understanding changed regarding how you are connected to what is around you? (p. 111)
- Which puzzling case puzzles you the most? (p. 124)
- Is the Collective Human Organism a viable concept? (p. 155)

How to Write and Tell Coincidence Stories

Coincidence stories teach us about each other and facilitate connecting with each other. The telling also illuminates hidden threads between you, your listeners, your readers, and nature. But the only way to do this is to tell each other coincidences stories![1]

You already have your own style of writing and telling stories. Get to know that part of yourself! When talking, how do you manage your primary nonverbals—facial: expressive or muted? Movements of arms and body: still or dynamic? Voice tone: dramatic, laid back, or somewhere in between? What is your preferred writing style—intellectual, clever, funny, precise, ambiguous, or something else entirely?

If this is the first time you are putting words on your experience, know that telling the story is like singing a song or reciting a joke. Better to have practiced it so you are in command of the flow and its details. The better you know the story, the more easily you can keep the audience in mind as you write or speak. You are striving to help them hear you as fully as possible.

But also keep in mind this key question: What details does the reader or listener *not* need to know?

You'll also want to keep in mind your general intent: to play the coincidence video running through your mind in the minds of the audience. Some results you might be trying to create are to:

- be reassured that you are not the only one experiencing something like this,
- convince someone of the reality of what you experienced,
- illuminate patterns in your own life, or
- encourage the listener or reader to tell or write their own stories.

Following are some general guidelines to help you tell the stories of your own coincidences.

General Format

- Title (the hook to get them interested, like online clickbait); options include:
    - A summary of the intersecting patterns,
    - A useful lesson of the story, or
    - An intriguing detail central to the story.
- Story
    - The structure of most coincidences involves two similar patterns coming together in a surprising, unexpected, low-probability way. Make the similar elements of the two patterns stand out clearly.
    - In describing the first pattern, emphasize the key aspects that you will later show to be repeated in the second pattern.
    - Convey how the coincidence is surprising or beyond expectations by emphasizing facts that lower the probability.
- Meaning. This can include:
    - The impact on you personally,
    - Your explanation, or
    - The category of coincidence (see the suggestions in several chapters of this book).
- Falsifications
    - To make stories sound better, tellers will sometimes add details that might not be true. That's why it's best to write down details of the story soon after the coincidence takes place. Coincidences resemble dreams. Both are hard to remember.

Tips for Writing
Who is your audience?

You? Load the stories up with the details that help you re-experience the emotions connected with the story.

People who know you? Include any and all details that help them get to know you better. The better they know you, the better they will resonate with details that you enjoy as ways to better get to know you.

Anonymous? Keep the story crisp, clear, and clean using only those details that expand the reader's immersion in your experience so they may feel some of your feeling.

Length

Generally speaking, this should not be more than half a page. Short is good for a quick, clear hit.

Write a longer story if there are interwoven elements that each contribute to the outcome.

You might think that the more detail you present, the more believable the coincidence is—the details demonstrate that you were really there!—but this is not necessarily true. You might include certain details because they carry you back into this memorable experience. But will those details resonate with your reader or listener?

Example

- Title: My dog got lost, I got lost, and we found each other
- Story: My dog Snapper ran away. My mother said go to the police station. The police did not know where he was. Blinded by my tears, I went the wrong way home and ran into Snapper.
- Personal Meaning: I needed that puppy! He was a lonely boy's best friend.
- Coincidence type: An example of human GPS
- Explanation: Getting to where I needed to be by getting lost, probably some form of psi

Tips for Telling
Imagine

The story is like a friend you are introducing to the audience. Maybe you can start with addressing the audience with something like: "Have you ever had a synchronicity that changed your life?"

Rehearse

Practice telling the story by writing it out or telling it to someone.

Time Yourself

Keep the length under three minutes; under two is better. Consider these key variables: how well you know the audience, how well they know you, and the number of people who will be listening.

A Final Word about Details

Whether you are writing or telling the story verbally, keep the details related to the coincidence itself, sharing only directly relevant details that your audience would enjoy as a way to know you better. Clearly communicate the patterns that shape the coincidence.

For the first time in his life Jim, age forty-five, told the following story, an example of excessive detail and its resolution.

He had gone to the University of Missouri-Columbia and stayed in Columbia. He gave a lot of details about his college roommates and trying to date someone who turned him down, and lists of dates he went on, and classes he took, and books he read, and the layout of the library where he tried to convince a certain young woman to go out with him.

He eventually got to describing how his two roommates helped him to go out with this reluctant young woman. She became friends with his two roommates, creating a marvelous, positive feeling for the foursome and each other. The reluctant young woman eventually became his wife.

He then described a visit soon after graduating to one roommate who was living in Australia and that man's problems with his wife.

He finally got to the coincidence itself, which took place in a national park, but described back entrances, wetlands, and other geographical features, and mixed in more details about his two roommates. He had not seen either roommate for over fifteen years. Then unexpectedly, surprisingly, both of them appeared at the same time at the same place in Yosemite National Park where he and his wife were celebrating their twentieth wedding anniversary.

His story took about five minutes to tell.

After re-booting his thinking, he was able to describe the patterns more clearly by removing the details from his account that were not directly relevant.

Setting: He and his wife went to Yosemite National Park in California for their twentieth wedding anniversary.

Pattern 1: He, his wife-to-be, and the two roommates were involved in an emotion-filled four-sided relationship that led to his marriage. He had not seen either roommate in many years although they had occasionally kept in touch. One lived in Florida and could only rarely leave the state because of his job. The other lived in Australia and had avoided coming to the United States.

Pattern 2: While crossing a bridge into the park, he heard his name being called. It was one of the roommates who then told him that the other roommate had just called to say hi and reported that he too was currently in the park. This event becomes a repetition of the original four-sided relationship that was instrumental in his marriage.

Meaning for him: The coincidence was highly meaningful to him because it further celebrated his marriage, which was the purpose of the trip.

My explanation: Running into people one knows in faraway places is more likely than it appears because people of the same socioeconomic status tend to visit similar places. That there were four people in a narrow time window meeting at the same place at an emotionally significant time lowers the probability significantly. Human GPS at work.

When you enthusiastically share your story, others will naturally become enthused by coincidences they spot or recall from their own lives. The emotion you generate will allow the reader or listener to connect emotionally as well as cognitively to you. The story the audience tells can also help clarify the meaning of your own coincidence. And it is likely that each of you will learn something new about the basic patterns from which meaningful coincidences are fashioned. You hopefully will contribute the stories to the coincidence research group for future analysis. And you are likely to discover things to inform our collective knowledge of meaningful coincidences.

Notes

CHAPTER I. ANATOMY OF A COINCIDENCE

1. Shepherd, "The History of Coincide and Coincidence."
2. Griffiths and Tenenbaum, "From Mere Coincidences to Meaningful Discoveries."
3. Maguire, Moser, Maguire, and Keane, "Seeing Patterns in Randomness."
4. Falk, "Judgment of Coincidences."
5. Falk and MacGregor, "The Surprisingness of Coincidences."
6. Johansen and Osman, "Coincidences: A Fundamental Consequence of Rational Cognition."
7. Coleman, Beitman, and Celebi, "Weird Coincidences Commonly Occur."
8. Combs and Holland, *Synchronicity.*
9. Beck, "The Most Common Kinds of Coincidences."

CHAPTER 2. TYPES OF COINCIDENCE

1. Jung, *Synchronicity.*
2. *Encyclopedia Britannica Online,* s.v. "J. B. Rhine," accessed November 12, 2020.
3. Jung, *Synchronicity,* 110.
4. Mansfield, *Synchronicity, Science and Soul-Making,* 27–34.
5. Main, "Energizing Jung's Ideas About Synchronicity."
6. Main, "Energizing Jung's Ideas About Synchronicity."
7. Jung, *Synchronicity.*
8. Main, "Energizing Jung's Ideas About Synchronicity."
9. Jung, *Synchronicity,* 96.
10. Main, *Jung on Synchronicity and the Paranormal,* 26–27.
11. Main, *Jung on Synchronicity and the Paranormal,* 27.

12. Cambray, *Synchronicity.*
13. Aziz, *C. G. Jung's Psychology of Religion and Synchronicity.*
14. Merton and Barber, *The Travels and Adventures of Serendipity.*
15. Austin, *Chase, Chance and Creativity,* 15.
16. Copeland, "On Serendipity in Science."
17. Merton and Barber, *The Travels and Adventures of Serendipity.*
18. Copeland, "On Serendipity in Science."
19. Copeland, "Was Fleming's Discovery of Penicillin a Paradigmatic Case of Serendipity, or Not?"
20. Meyers, *Happy Accidents.*
21. Lakshminarayanan, "Roentgen and His Rays."
22. Van Andel, "Anatomy of the Unsought Finding."
23. Meyers, *Happy Accidents.*
24. The Serendipity Society website.
25. Koestler, *The Case of the Midwife Toad,* appendix 1.
26. Koestler, *The Case of the Midwife Toad,* appendix 1.
27. Kammerer, *Das Gesetz der Serie, eine Lehre von den Wiederholungen im Lebens und im Weltgeschehen.*
28. Playfair, *Twin Telepathy,* 37–38; Mann and Jaye, "'Are We One Body?'"
29. Stevenson, *Telepathic Impressions,* 17–22.
30. Coleman, Beitman, and Celebi, "Weird Coincidences Commonly Occur."
31. Stevenson, *Telepathic Impressions,* 16.
32. T. Hamilton, s.v. "Frederic WH Myers," *Psi Encyclopedia Online* (London: Society for Psychical Research, 2017), accessed November 11, 2020.
33. Jung, *Memories Dreams and Reflections,* 137–38.
34. Playfair, *Twin Telepathy,* 37–38; Mann and Jaye, "'Are We One Body?'"
35. Schwarz, "Possible Telesomatic Reactions."
36. Dossey, "Unbroken Wholeness."

CHAPTER 3. PATTERNS OF COINCIDENCE

1. Nguyen, "Don't Forget: The Plural of Anecdote Is Data."
2. "What Are Black Swan Events?" Black Swan website: http://black swanevents.org.
3. Ironmonger, "Novelist and Coincidences."
4. Jackson, "49 Birds Appear over Orlando Shooting Victims Memorial."
5. Jung, *Synchronicity,* 22.

6. Grof, "An Interview with Stanislav Grof."

7. Halberstam and Leventhal, *Small Miracles from Beyond,* 228–31.

8. Coleman, Beitman, and Celebi, "Weird Coincidences Commonly Occur."

9. Spacek, *My Ordinary, Extraordinary Life,* 180–85.

10. Obama White House, "Behind the Lens."

11. "In Memoriam: Elisabeth Targ (1961–2002)," the Parapsychological Association website, accessed April 26, 2020. Site no longer accessible; Targ, "Evaluating Distant Healing."

12. Inglis, *Coincidence,* 94.

13. M. Robertson, *Futility, or The Wreck of the Titan* (New York: M. F. Mansfield, 1898); Wikipedia s.v. "Futility, or the Wreck of the Titan."

14. Stevenson, "Precognition of Disasters."

15. Mann and Jaye, "'Are We One body?'"

16. Guy L. Playfair, s.v. "Twin Telepathy," *Psi Encyclopedia* (London: Society for Psychical Research, 2015), accessed August 15, 2020.

17. Playfair, "Twin Telepathy."

18. Playfair, *Twin Telepathy,* 61.

19. Brown and Sheldrake, "The Anticipation of Telephone Calls."

20. Sheldrake and Smart, "Experimental Tests for Telephone Telepathy."

21. Rushnell, *When God Winks on Love,* 44–47.

22. Inglis, *Coincidence,* 116.

23. Inglis, *Coincidence,* 116.

24. Jung, *Synchronicity,* 27.

25. Stevenson, *Telepathic Impressions,* 31–34.

26. Freud, "Dreams and Occultism," 31–56.

27. Silverman, "Correspondences and Thought-Transference During Psychoanalysis."

28. Anthony, *Discover Your Soul Template,* 113–16; Anthony, "Classroom Coincidences."

29. Goldman, "From the Annals of the Strange."

30. Berne, *When the Horses Whisper.*

31. Storey, Walsh, Quinton, and Wynne-Edwards, "Hormonal Correlates of Paternal Responsiveness in New and Expectant Fathers."

32. Feather and Schmicker, *The Gift,* 91.

33. Mann and Jaye, "'Are We One Body?'

34. Ogburn and Thomas, "Are Inventions Inevitable?"

35. Baily, "The Odd Case of Dennis the Menace."

36. Schwartz, *Super Synchronicity.*

37. Sparks, "Study Guide for Marie-Louise Von Franz's Number and Time."

38. Rushnell, *When God Winks on Love,* 93–96.

39. Anonymous personal communication.

40. McLaughlin and Zagon, "POMC-Derived Opioid Peptides."

41. Alger, "Getting High on the Endocannabinoid System," 14.

42. Plimmer and King, *Beyond Coincidence,* 116–17.

43. Charles Dickens, *A Tale of Two Cities,* edited by Richard Maxwell (London: Penguin Classics, 2003; first published in 1859).

44. Weaver, *Lady Luck;* Hardy, Harvie, and Koestler, *The Challenge of Chance,* 214–15.

45. Rumi, "A Great Wagon."

CHAPTER 4. COINCIDENCE SENSITIVITY

1. Coleman, Beitman, and Celebi, "Weird Coincidences Commonly Occur."

2. Coleman and Beitman, "Characterizing High-Frequency Coincidence Detectors."

3. Costin, Dzara, and Resch, "Synchronicity"; Attig, Schwartz, Figueredo, Jacobs, and Bryson, "Coincidences, Intuition, and Spirituality"; Coleman and Beitman, "Characterizing High-Frequency Coincidence Detectors."

4. Jones, "About the Free Associations Method."

5. Jung, "What Is Active Imagination."

6. Björneborn, "Three Key Affordances for Serendipity."

7. Deikman, *The Observing Self.*

8. "Pattern Recognition (Physiological Psychology)," Psychology Wiki.

9. Festinger, Riecken, and Schachter, *When Prophecy Fails.*

10. Beitman, *Connecting with Coincidence.*

11. Mind Tools Content Team, "The Holmes and Rahe Stress Scale," MindTools website, accessed in 2020.

12. Noone, "The Holmes–Rahe Stress Inventory."

13. Björneborn, "Three Key Affordances for Serendipity."

CHAPTER 5. A STATISTICIAN'S APPROACH

1. "Lightning: Victim Data," Centers for Disease Control and Prevention website.

2. "The Strange, Sad Story of Roy Cleveland Sullivan," QuickMedical website, September 27, 2010. Site no longer accessible.

3. Wright, Phillips, Whalley, Choo, Ng, Tan, et al., "Cultural Differences in Probabilistic Thinking."

4. Science Buddies, "Probability and the Birthday Paradox."

5. "Apophenia," Merriam Webster Dictionary online.

6. Van Elk, Friston, and Bekkering, "The Experience of Coincidence."

7. "Mike Myers + Deepak Chopra Coincidences Clip," Iconoclasts (S3), YouTube. Video no longer available.

8. Johansen and Osman, "Coincidences"; Johansen and Osman, "Coincidence Judgment in Causal Reasoning."

9. Diaconis and Mosteller, "Methods of Studying Coincidences."

10. Lewis, "Coming to Terms with Coincidence."

11. Black, "McKay Takes Math beyond Moonshine."

12. Rawlette, "How Skeptics Misapply the Law of Very Large Numbers."

13. Hand, *The Improbability Principle.*

14. Wikipedia s.v. "Roy Sullivan."

CHAPTER 6. SIGNS FROM GOD

1. Coleman, Beitman, and Celebi, "Weird Coincidences Commonly Occur."

2. Rawlette, *The Source and Significance of Coincidences,* 43.

3. Rushnell, *Godwinks.*

4. Elizabeth Gilbert, *Eat, Pray, Love: One Woman's Search for Everything Across Italy, India and Indonesia* (New York: Viking, 2006), 30–34.

5. Godevenos, *Human Resources for the Church.*

6. Ken Godevenos email to Bernard Beitman, April 22, 2017.

7. Lynne, *Coincide,* 31–36.

8. Rawlette, "Are Coincidences Signs from God?"

CHAPTER 7. PERSONAL AGENCY

1. Purves, Augustine, Fitzpatrick, et al., "Types of Eye Movements and Their Functions."

2. Blackmore and Chamberlain, "ESP and Thought Concordance in Twins."

3. Williams, *Demystifying Meaningful Coincidences (Synchronicities).*

4. Gibbs Williams email to Bernard Beitman, May 23, 2020.

5. Erdelez, "Information Encountering."

6. Austin, *Chase, Chance, and Creativity,* 73–74.

7. Kelly, "We Called Her 'Moldy Mary.'"

8. "The Nobel Prize in Physiology or Medicine 1945," the Nobel Prize website.

9. Jung, *Synchronicity*.

CHAPTER 8. HUMAN GPS

1. Winston Churchill, *My Early Life* (New York: Touchstone, 1930), 280–81.

2. Cardeña, "The Experimental Evidence for Parapsychological Phenomena."

3. Cardeña, "The Experimental Evidence for Parapsychological Phenomena."

4. Stanford, Zennhausern, Taylor, and Dwyer, "Psychokinesis as a Psi-Mediated Instrumental Response."

5. Michael Duggan, s.v. "Rex G Stanford," *Psi Encyclopedia* (London: Society for Psychical Research, 2020), accessed August 15, 2020.

6. Stanford and Stio, "Associative Mediation in Psi-Mediated Instrumental Response (PMIR)"; Palmer, "The Challenge of Experimenter."

7. Wood, "Neuroscience Researchers Receive $3.4 Million NIH Grant to Develop Brain-Controlled Prosthetic Limbs."

CHAPTER 9. PROBLEMATIC COINCIDENCES

1. Masters, *Spiritual Bypassing*.

2. Swain, "How Do We Go Palm Oil Free?"

3. Roberts, "Herman Rosenblat, 85, Dies: Made Up Holocaust Love Story."

4. Jones, *Let Me Take You Down*.

5. Goodstein, "Falwell: Blame Abortionists, Feminists and Gays."

6. Mattingly, "Religion News Service Offers Readers One Half of the 'Why Did God Smite Houston?' story."

7. Blumenfield, "God and Natural Disasters."

8. WorldTribune Staff, "Coincidence?"

9. Smurzyńska, "The Role of Emotions in Delusion Formation."

10. Beitman, "The Manic Psychiatrist's Experience of Synchronicity."

11. Beitman, "Is a Flood of Coincidences Challenging Your Sanity?"

12. Beitman, "Is a Flood of Coincidences Challenging Your Sanity?"

13. Beitman, "The Manic Psychiatrist's Experience of Synchronicity."

14. Wimmer, *A Second in Eternity*.

15. Beitman, "Research Suggests That Synchronicities Can Aid Psychotherapy."

CHAPTER 10. COINCIDER TYPES

1. Mishlove, "Jeffrey Mishlove: Progress in Parapsychology."
2. Engen, "A Triple Coincidence Enhances His Life."
3. Sharon Hewitt Rawlette email to Bernard Beitman, August 28, 2020.
4. Burger and Anderson, "What a Coincidence!"
5. Erdelez, "Information Encountering."
6. Gertz, "Be a Super-Encounterer."
7. Jaworski, *Synchronicity.*
8. Generon International website s.v. "Joseph Jaworski." Site no longer available.
9. Bache, *The Living Classroom,* ch. 1 "Resonance in the Classroom."
10. Roxburgh, Ridgway, and Roe, "Issue 2: The Use of Qualitative Research in Developing Users' and Providers' Perspectives in the Psychological Therapies."
11. Brandon, *Synchronicity.*
12. Keutzer, "Synchronicity in Psychotherapy."
13. Reefschläger, "Synchronizität in der Psychotherapie" [Dissertation: Synchronicity in Psychotherapy].
14. Hopcke, *There Are No Accidents.*
15. Roesler and Reefschläger, "Jungian Psychotherapy, Spirituality, and Synchronicity."
16. Marlo and Kline, "Synchronicity and Psychotherapy."
17. Zylstra, "Moments That Matter."
18. Boris Pasternak, *Doctor Zhivago* (London: Vintage, 2011, translated by Richard Pevear and Larissa Volokhonsky), letter in English, February 8, 1959, page xiii.
19. Forsyth, "Wonderful Chains."
20. Dannenberg, "A Poetics of Coincidence in Narrative Fiction"; Browne, "Coincidence in Fiction and Literature."
21. Hand, *The Improbability Principle.*
22. Ironmonger, *Coincidence* (also called *The Coincidence Authority*).
23. Ironmonger, "Novelist and Coincidences,"
24. Lewis, "Coming to Terms with Coincidence."
25. Beitman, "Can Mainstream Science Be Expanded to Study Coincidences?"
26. Stenger, *Quantum Gods.*
27. Csikszentmihalyi, *Flow.*
28. Singer, *The Surrender Experiment.*
29. Nelson-Isaacs, *Living in Flow.*

30. Rushnell, "Godwinks History" and *Godwinks* books.

31. Perry, *Signs,* 28–29.

32. Lindorff and Fierz, *Pauli and Jung.*

33. Clayton, "Conceptual Foundations of Emergence Theory."

34. Rickles, Hawe, and Shiell, "A Simple Guide to Chaos and Complexity."

35. Rickles, Hawe, and Shiell, "A Simple Guide to Chaos and Complexity."

36. "What are Fractals?" The Fractal Foundation website.

37. Marks-Tarlow, "A Fractal Epistemology for Transpersonal Psychology."

38. Cambray, "Moments of Complexity and Enigmatic Action."

39. Copeland, "On Serendipity in Science."

40. Sacco, "Dynamical and Statistical Modeling of Synchronicity"; Sacco, "Fibonacci Harmonics."

41. Schwartz, *Super Synchronicity.*

42. Milmo and Willetts, "23 Fascinating Facts about the Number Twenty-Three."

CHAPTER 11. "THERE ARE NO COINCIDENCES"

1. Townley and Schmidt, "Paul Kammerer and the Law of Seriality."

2. Jung, *Synchronicity,* 9.

3. Schwartz, *Super Synchronicity.*

4. Stenger, *Quantum Gods.*

5. Schwartz, *Super Synchronicity.*

6. Horgan, "Scientific Heretic Rupert Sheldrake on Morphic Fields, Psychic Dogs and Other Mysteries."

7. Horgan, "Scientific Heretic Rupert Sheldrake on Morphic Fields, Psychic Dogs and Other Mysteries."

CHAPTER 12. FROM UNUS MUNDUS TO THE PSYCHOSPHERE

1. Jung, *Collected Works of C.G. Jung, Volume 14,* excerpted by Roderick Main in *Jung on Synchronicity and the Paranormal,* 165.

2. Jung, *Collected Works of C.G. Jung,* Vol. 9 (Part 1).

3. Jung, *Collected Works of C.G. Jung,* Vol. 9 (Part 1), 275.

4. Dossey, *One Mind.*

5. Kelly, Kelly, Crabtree, Gross, and Greyson, *Irreducible Mind*.

6. Wise, "When Fear Makes Us Superhuman"; Wikipedia, s.v. "Hysterical strength."

7. Dossey, *One Mind*, 165–66.

8. Beitman, *Connecting with Coincidence*.

9. Gauld, "Reflections on the Life and Work of Ian Stevenson," 31.

10. Sire, *Discipleship of the Mind*, 46.

11. "Biosphere," definition from the National Geographic website.

12. Christian, "The Noösphere"; Ockham, "The Noosphere."

13. Cole, "The Concept of Collective Consciousness."

14. Todeschi, "Edgar Cayce on the Akashic Record."

15. Bateson, *Steps to an Ecology of Mind*, 467.

16. Breslow, "What Does Solitary Confinement Do to Your Mind?"

17. Keirle-Smith, *Revelation Antarctica*.

18. Ogburn and Thomas, "Are Inventions Inevitable?"

19. Gilbert, *Big Magic;* Paskin, "Elizabeth Gilbert's 'Big Magic.'"

20. Harris, *Simulpathity*.

21. Beitman, "As Above, So Below."

22. Beitman, "Are We Becoming Nodes in the Vast Internet Connectivity?"

CHAPTER 13. SIX PUZZLING CASES

1. "History of Magnetism," Science Encyclopedia website.

2. Rawlette, *The Source and Significance of Coincidences*, 1–2.

3. Roger Nelson s.v. "Princeton Engineering Anomalies Research (PEAR)," *Psi Encyclopedia* (London: Society for Psychical Research, 2017), accessed August 15, 2020.

4. Rawlette email to Bernard Beitman, October 22, 2019.

5. Rawlette, *The Source and Significance of Coincidences*, 430.

6. "Balloon Coincidence Weird Unusual Story," posted by Media Digital; "Most Amazing Coincidence Ever," posted by Good Mythical Morning; "Strange Coincidences or Destiny Beyond Chance?" posted by Richard Gardner.

7. "Incroyables Coïncidences," posted by Fabrice Bolusset.

8. "A Very Lucky Wind," *RadioLab* podcast.

9. Shermer, "Anomalous Events That Can Shake One's Skepticism to the Core."

10. Shermer, "Anomalous Events That Can Shake One's Skepticism to the Core."

11. Shermer, "Do Anomalies Prove the Existence of God?"

12. "Adam Trombly Recalls Stories of John C. Lilly," *Float* podcast.

13. Rawlette, *The Source and Significance of Coincidences,* chapter 8.

14. "E.C.C.O.," John C. Lilly Home Page.

15. Scharf, "The Solar Eclipse Coincidence."

16. Powell, "Earth's Moon Destined to Disintegrate."

17. Scharf, "The Solar Eclipse Coincidence."

18. Smith, "Why Is the Moon Exactly the Same Apparent Size from Earth as the Sun?"

19. Knight and Butler, *Who Built the Moon?*

20. Jung, Adler (ed.), Hulen (trans.), *Letters C. G. Jung,* 45.

21. Kelly, Kelly, Crabtree, Gross, and Greyson, *Irreducible Mind;* Michael Grosso email to Bernard Beitman, November 23, 2020.

CHAPTER 14. THE PRACTICAL USES OF COINCIDENCES

1. Prochaska and DiClemente, "Stages and Processes of Self-Change of Smoking."

2. Herron, "People Are Losing It Over #UberBae's Sordid Side-Chick Tale of Betrayal."

3. Tarnas, *Cosmos and Psyche,* 54.

4. Nelson-Isaacs, *Leap to Wholeness,* 20.

5. Gorman, "Grid Cells."

6. Hill, "Synchronicity and Grief."

7. Irvine, *Infinite Possibility.*

8. Cardeña, "The Experimental Evidence for Parapsychological Phenomena."

9. Björneborn, "Three Key Affordances for Serendipity."

10. Small, "The Formula for Successful."

11. Kidd and Hayden, "The Psychology and Neuroscience of Curiosity."

12. Deikman, *The Observing Self.*

13. Leary, "Interpersonal Circle Model of Personality."

14. Beitman and Viamontes, "Unconscious Role-Induction."

A PERSONAL POSTSCRIPT: THE COLLECTIVE HUMAN ORGANISM

1. Harari, *Sapiens*.
2. Grosso, *The Millennium Myth*.

APPENDIX 1: THE COINCIDENCE PROJECT

1. Beitman, "The Five Most Common Coincidences."
2. Coleman, Beitman, and Celebi, "Weird Coincidences Commonly Occur."
3. Costin, Dzara, and Resch, "Synchronicity."
4. Greyson, "Meaningful Coincidence and Near-Death Experiences."
5. Hill, "Synchronicity and Grief."
6. "Synchro Summit at Yale," Synchro Summit.

APPENDIX 2: HOW TO WRITE AND TELL COINCIDENCE STORIES

1. Stockbridge and Wooffitt, "Coincidence by Design." To my knowledge this appendix is the most detailed advice about how to tell coincidence stories. Stockbridge and Wooffit (2018) may have been among the first to make concrete suggestions.

Bibliography

"Adam Trombly Recalls Stories of John C Lilly." *Float* podcast. Sep 4, 2015. YouTube.

Alger, B. E. "Getting High on the Endocannabinoid System. *Cerebrum* (2013), 14.

Anthony, Marcus. *Discover Your Soul Template: 14 Steps for Awakening Integrated Intelligence*. Rochester, Vt.: Inner Traditions, 2012.

———. "Classroom Coincidences." *Connecting with Coincidence with Dr. Bernard Beitman* podcast, June 6, 2019. Available on Spreaker.

Attig, Sheryl, Gary E. Schwartz, Aurelio Jose Figueredo, W. Jake Jacobs, and K. C. Bryson. "Coincidences, Intuition, and Spirituality." *Psychiatric Annals* 41, no. 12 (December 2011).

Austin, James. *Chase, Chance, and Creativity*. Cambridge, Mass.: MIT Press, 1978, 2003.

"A Very Lucky Wind," *RadioLab* podcast, June 15, 2009.

Aziz, Robert. *C. G. Jung' Psychology of Religion and Synchronicity*. Albany: State University of New York Press, 1990.

Bache, Christopher. *The Living Classroom: Teaching and Collective Consciousness*. Albany: State University of New York Press, 2008.

Baily, Jonathan. "The Odd Case of Dennis the Menace." Plagiarism Today website, October 18, 2010.

"Balloon Coincidence Weird Unusual Story," *Media Digital,* April 1, 2008. YouTube.

Bateson, Gregory. *Steps to an Ecology of Mind*. San Francisco: Chandler Press, 1972.

Beck, Julie. "The Most Common Kinds of Coincidences." *Atlantic,* May 6, 2016.

Beitman, Bernard. "Are We Becoming Nodes in the Vast Internet Connectivity?" Connecting with Coincidence blog, *Psychology Today,* Nov 30, 2016.

———. "As Above, So Below—A Sky-Brain Coincidence," Connecting with Coincidence blog, *Psychology Today,* January 12, 2017.

———. "Can Mainstream Science Be Expanded to Study Coincidences?" Connecting with Coincidence blog, *Psychology Today,* April 30, 2020.

———. *Connecting with Coincidence.* Deerfield Beach, Fla.: Health Communications, 2016.

———. *Connecting with Coincidence* podcast. Available on Spreaker, YouTube, and the author's website coincider.com.

———. "The Five Most Common Coincidences: Two Statistical Approaches with Overlapping Outcomes." Connecting with Coincidence blog, *Psychology Today,* June 18, 2016.

———. "Is a Flood of Coincidences Challenging Your Sanity?" Connecting with Coincidence blog, *Psychology Today,* December 11, 2016.

———. "The Manic Psychiatrist's Experience of Synchronicity." Connecting with Coincidence blog, *Psychology Today,* August 16, 2018.

———. "Research Suggests That Synchronicities Can Aid Psychotherapy." Connecting with Coincidence blog, *Psychology Today,* November 25, 2020.

Beitman, Bernard D., and George I. Viamontes. "Unconscious Role-Induction: Implications for Psychotherapy." *Psychiatric Annals* 37, no. 4 (2007).

Berne, Rosalyn. *When the Horses Whisper: The Wisdom of Wise and Sentient Beings.* Rainbow Ridge Books, 2013.

Björneborn, Lennart. "Three Key Affordances for Serendipity: Toward a Framework Connecting Environmental and Personal Factors in Serendipitous Encounters." *Journal of Documentation* 73, no. 5 (September 11, 2017): 1053–81.

Black, Barbara. "McKay Takes Math beyond Moonshine." *Concordia Journal,* April 19, 2007.

Blackmore, S. J., and F. Chamberlain. "ESP and Thought Concordance in Twins. A Method of Comparison." *Journal of the Society of Psychical Research* 59 (1993): 89–96.

Blumenfield, Warren. "God and Natural Disasters: It's the Gays' Fault?" *HuffPost,* February 2, 2016.

Brandon, Nathan. *Synchronicity: A Phenomenological Study of Jungian Analysts' Lived Experience of Meaningful Coincidence in the Context of Psychotherapy,* California Institute of Integral Studies: San Francisco, Calif., 2015.

Breslow, Jason M. "What Does Solitary Confinement Do to Your Mind?" Frontline website, April 22, 2014.

Brown, D and R. Sheldrake. "The Anticipation of Telephone Calls: A Survey in California." *Journal of Parapsychology* 65 (2001): 145–56.

Browne, L. "Coincidence in Fiction and Literature." *Australian Journal of Parapsychology* 19. no. 1 (2019): 45–75.

Burger, Jerry M., and Carmen Anderson. "What a Coincidence! The Effects of Incidental Similarity on Compliance." *Personality & Social Psychology Bulletin,* March 20, 2004.

Cambray, Joseph. "Moments of Complexity and Enigmatic Action: A Jungian View of the Therapeutic Field" *Journal of Analytical Psychology,* June 2011.

———. *Synchronicity: Nature and Psyche in an Interconnected Universe.* College Station: Texas A & M University Press, 2009.

Cardeña, E., "The Experimental Evidence for Parapsychological Phenomena: A Review." *American Psychologist* 73, no. 5 (2018): 663–77.

Chase, James Austin. *Chance and Creativity: The Lucky Art of Novelty.* Cambridge, Mass.: MIT Press, 2003.

Christian, David. "The Noösphere," response to "What Scientific Term Or Concept Ought To Be More Widely Known?" Edge website 2017.

Clayton, P. "Conceptual Foundations of Emergence Theory." In *The Re-emergence of Emergence,* edited by P. Clayton and P. Davies, 1–31. Oxford: Oxford University Press, 2006.

Cole, Nicki Lisa. "The Concept of Collective Consciousness." ThoughtCo website, June 5, 2019.

Coleman, S. L., and B. D. Beitman. "Characterizing High-Frequency Coincidence Detectors." *Psychiatric Annals* 39, no. 5 (2009): 271–79.

Coleman, S. L., B. D. Beitman, and E. Celebi. "Weird Coincidences Commonly Occur." *Psychiatric Annals* 39 (2009): 265–70.

Combs, A. and M. Holland. *Synchronicity: Through the Eyes of Science, Myth and the Trickster.* New York: Marlow and Company, 1996.

Copeland, S. "On Serendipity in Science: Discovery at the Intersection of Chance and Wisdom." *Synthese* 196 (2019): 2385–406.

Copeland, Samantha. "Was Fleming's Discovery of Penicillin a Paradigmatic Case of Serendipity, or Not?" *Semantic Scholar* (2016).

Costin, George, Kristina Dzara, and David Resch. "Synchronicity: Coincidence Detection and Meaningful Life Events." *Psychiatric Annals* 41, no. 12 (December 2011): 572–75.

Csikszentmihalyi, Mihaly. *Flow: The Psychology of Optimal Experience.* New York: Harper Perennial Classics, 2008.

Dannenberg, H. P. "A Poetics of Coincidence in Narrative Fiction." *Poetics Today* 25, no. 3 (2004): 399–436.

Deikman, Arthur. *The Observing Self: Mysticism and Psychotherapy.* Boston, Mass.: Beacon Books, 1982.

Diaconis, Persi, and Frederick Mosteller. "Methods of Studying Coincidences." *Journal of the American Statistical Association* 84, no. 408 (December 1989): 853–61.

Dossey, Larry. *One Mind: How Our Individual Mind Is Part of a Greater Consciousness and Why It Matters.* Carlsbad, Calif.: Hay House, 2013.

———. "Unbroken Wholeness: The Emerging View of Human Interconnectedness." Reality Sandwich website, March 13, 2013.

"E.C.C.O. page." John C. Lilly Home Page, johnclilly.com.

Engen, Brendan. "A Triple Coincidence Enhances His Life," Connecting with Coincidence blog, *Psychology Today,* January 12, 2018.

Erdelez, Sanda. "Information Encountering." In *Theories of Information Behavior* edited by K. E. Fisher, S. Erdelez, and L. McKechnie, 179–85. Medford, N.J.: Information Today, 2005.

Falk, R. "Judgment of Coincidences: Mine vs. Yours." *American Journal of Psychology* 102 (1989): 477–93.

Falk, R., and D. MacGregor. "The Surprisingness of Coincidences." In *Analysing and Aiding Decision Processes,* edited by P. Humphreys, O. Svenson, and A. Vari, 489–502. Budapest: Akadémiai Kiadó, 1983.

Feather, Sally Rhine, and Michael Schmicker. *The Gift: ESP, the Extraordinary Experiences of Ordinary People.* New York: St. Martin's Press, 2006.

Festinger, L., H. W. Riecken, and S. Schachter. *When Prophecy Fails.* Chicago: Pinter & Martin Publishers, 2008.

Forsyth, Neil. "Wonderful Chains: Dickens and Coincidence." *Modern Philology* 83, no. 2 (November 1985): 151–65.

Freud, S. "Dreams and Occultism." *New Introductory Lectures on Psychoanalysis* Standard Edition (1932), Vol. 22, 1933, pp 31–56.

Gauld, Alan. "Reflections on the Life and Work of Ian Stevenson." *Journal of Scientific Exploration* 22, no. 1 (2008): 31.

Gertz, Geoffry. "Be a Super-Encounterer." Geoffry Gertz website.

Gilbert, Elizabeth. *Big Magic: Creative Living beyond Fear.* New York: Penguin, 2016.

Godevenos, Ken B. *Human Resources for the Church: Applying Corporate Practices in a Spiritual Setting.* Belleville, Ontario: Essence Publishing, 2009.

Goldman, Jason G. "From the Annals of the Strange: Dog Telepathy." The Thoughtful Animal blog, *Scientific American,* February 7, 2011.

Goodstein, Laurie. "Falwell: Blame Abortionists, Feminists and Gays." *Guardian,* September 19, 2001.

Gorman, James. "Grid Cells: 'Crystals of the Brain.'" *New York Times,* April 29, 2013.

Greyson, Bruce. "Meaningful Coincidence and Near-Death Experiences." *Psychiatric Annals* 41, no. 12 (December 2011).

Griffiths, T. L., and J. B. Tenenbaum. "From Mere Coincidences to Meaningful Discoveries." *Cognition* 103, no. 2 (May 2007): 180–226.

Grof, Stanislav. "An Interview with Stanislav Grof" by Janice Hughes and Dennis Hughes. Share Guide website.

Grosso, Michael. *The Millennium Myth: Love and Death at the End of Time.* New York: Random House, 1997.

Halberstam, Yitta, and Judith Leventhal. *Small Miracles from Beyond.* New York: Sterling Ethos, 2014.

Hand, David J. *The Improbability Principle: Why Coincidences, Miracles, and Rare Events Happen Every Day.* New York: Scientific American, 2014.

Harari, Yuval Noah. *Sapiens: A Brief History of Humankind.* New York: Harper Collins, 2015.

Hardy, Alister, Robert Harvie, and Arthur Koestler. *The Challenge of Chance: A Mass Experiment in Telepathy and Its Unexpected Outcome.* London: Hutchinson, 1973.

Harris, Parker. *Simulpathity*, 2016. Available on Vimeo.

Herron, Rachel. "People Are Losing It Over #UberBae's Sordid Side-Chick Tale of Betrayal." *BET,* March 29, 2017.

Hill, Jennifer. "Synchronicity and Grief: The Phenomenology of Meaningful Coincidence as It Arises During Bereavement." Institute of Transpersonal Psychology, March 14, 2011.

Hopcke, Robert. *There Are No Accidents: Synchronicity and the Stories of Our Lives.* New York: Riverhead Books, 1998.

Horgan, John. "Scientific Heretic Rupert Sheldrake on Morphic Fields, Psychic Dogs and Other Mysteries." Cross Check blog, *Scientific American,* July 14, 2014.

"Incroyables Coïncidences." Fabrice Bolusset. June 30, 2015. Youtube.

Inglis, Brian. *Coincidence.* London: Hutchinson, 1990.

Ironmonger, John. *Coincidence* (also called *The Coincidence Authority*). New York: Harper Perennial, 2014.

————. "John Ironmonger: Novelist and Coincidences." *Connecting with Coincidence with Bernard Beitman* podcast October 31, 2019. Available on Spreaker.

Irvine, Audrey. *Infinite Possibility: Frameworks for Understanding Extraordinary Human Experience.* Bloomington, Ind.: Author House, 2008.

Jackson, Amanda. "49 Birds Appear over Orlando Shooting Victims Memorial." *CNN,* June 14, 2016.

Jaworski, Joseph. *Synchronicity: The Inner Path of Leadership.* Berrett-Koehler Publishers, 2011.

Johansen, Mark K., and Magda Osman. "Coincidences: A Fundamental Consequence of Rational Cognition." *New Ideas in Psychology* 39 (2015): 34–44.

————. "Coincidence Judgment in Causal Reasoning: How Coincidental Is This?" *Cognitive Psychology* 120 (August 2020): 101290.

Jones, J. "About the Free Associations Method," FreudFile website.

Jones, Jack. *Let Me Take You Down: Inside the Mind of Mark David Chapman, the Man Who Killed John Lennon.* New York: Villard, 1992.

Jung, Carl. *Collected Works of C.G. Jung.* Vol. 9 (Part 1), *Archetypes and the Collective Unconscious.* Princeton, N.J.: Princeton University Press, 1969.

————. *Collected Works of C.G. Jung.* Vol. 14, *Mysterium Coniunctionis.* Princeton, N.J.: Princeton University Press, 1997.

————. *Memories Dreams and Reflections.* New York: Vintage Books, 1963.

————. *Synchronicity.* Princeton, N.J.: Princeton Press, 1973.

————. "What Is Active Imagination," *The Conjunction,* CW 14, par. 706.

Jung, Carl. *Letters C.G. Jung.* edited by Gerhard Adler, translated by Jeffrey Hulen. Vol. 2, 1951–1961. London: Routledge & Kegan Paul, 1976.

Kammerer, Paul. *Das Gesetz der Serie, eine Lehre von den Wiederholungen im Lebens und im Weltgeschehen.* Stuttgart und Berlin, 1919.

Keirle-Smith, Gordon. *Revelation Antarctica.* Paradise Garden Press, 2019.

Kelly, Edward, Emily Kelly, Adam Crabtree, Michael Gross, and Bruce Greyson. *Irreducible Mind: Toward a Psychology for the 21st Century.* Lanham, Md.: Rowman and Littlefield, 2009.

Kelly, Norman V. "We Called Her 'Moldy Mary.'" Peoria Historian blog, April 20, 2013.

Keutzer, Caroline S. "Synchronicity in Psychotherapy." *Journal of Analytic Psychology* 29, no. 4 (1984): 373–81.

Kidd, Celeste, and Benjamin Y. Hayden. "The Psychology and Neuroscience of Curiosity." *Neuron* 88, no. 3 (2015): 449–60.

Knight, Christopher, and Alan Butler. *Who Built the Moon?* London: Watkins, 2007.

Koestler, Arthur. *The Case of the Midwife Toad.* New York: Random House, 1971.

Lakshminarayanan, V. "Roentgen and His Rays." *Resonance* 10, no. 6 (June 2005): 2–5.

Leary, Timothy. "Interpersonal Circle Model of Personality." PAEI—Structures of Concern website.

Lewis, Ralph. "Coming to Terms with Coincidence." *Psychology Today,* February 13, 2020 (reviewed March 2020).

Lindorff, David, and Markus Fierz. *Pauli and Jung: The Meeting of Two Great Minds.* Wheaton, Ill.: Quest Books, 2004.

Lynne, Sherrie. *Coincide: A Two Bits Testimony.* Sioux Falls, S.Dak.: Gimmel Publishing, 2020.

Maguire, P., P. Moser, R. Maguire, and M. T. Keane. "Seeing Patterns in Randomness: A Computational Model of Surprise." *Topics in Cognitive Science* 11, no. 1 (2019): 103–18.

Main, Roderick. "Energizing Jung's Ideas About Synchronicity." Connecting with Coincidence blog, *Psychology Today,* May 2017.

———. *Jung on Synchronicity and the Paranormal.* Princeton, N.J.: Princeton University Press, 1997.

Mann, Brett, and Chrystal Jaye. "'Are We One Body?' Body Boundaries in Telesomatic Experiences." *Anthropology & Medicine* 14, no. 2 (August 2007): 183–95.

Mansfield, Victor. *Synchronicity, Science and Soul-Making: Understanding Jungian Synchronicity through Physics, Buddhism and Philosophy.* Chicago and La Salle, Ill.: Open Court, 1995.

Marks-Tarlow, Terry. "A Fractal Epistemology for Transpersonal Psychology." *International Journal of Transpersonal Studies* 39, no. 1 (2020).

Marlo, Helen, and Jeffrey Kline, "Synchronicity and Psychotherapy: Unconscious Communication in the Psychotherapeutic Relationship." *Psychotherapy* 35, no. 1 (Spring 1998): 16–22.

Masters, Robert. *Spiritual Bypassing: When Spirituality Disconnects Us from What Really Matters.* Berkeley: North Atlantic, 2010.

Mattingly, Terry. "Religion News Service Offers Readers One Half of the 'Why Did God Smite Houston?' Story." Get Religion website, August 30, 2017.

McLaughlin, Patricia J., and Ian S. Zagon. "POMC-Derived Opioid Peptides." *Handbook of Biologically Active Peptides.* 2nd ed., edited by Abba J. Kastin. San Diego: Academic Press, 2013.

Merton, Robert K., and Elinor Barber. *The Travels and Adventures of Serendipity.* Princeton, N.J.: Princeton Press, 2004.

Meyers, Morton A. *Happy Accidents: Serendipity in Modern Medical Breakthroughs.* New York: Arcade Publishing, 2007.

Milmo, Cahal, and Tom Willetts. "23 Fascinating Facts about the Number Twenty-Three." *Independent,* February 23, 2007.

Mishlove, Jeffrey. "Jeffrey Mishlove: Progress in Parapsychology." *Connecting with Coincidence with Dr. Bernard Beitman* podcast, January 29, 2018. Available on Spreaker.

"Most Amazing Coincidence Ever." *Good Mythical Morning.* June 16, 2014, season 5, episode 112. Youtube.

Nelson-Isaacs, Sky. *Leap to Wholeness: How the World Is Programmed to Help Us Grow, Heal, and Adapt.* Berkeley: North Atlantic Books, 2021.

———. *Living in Flow: The Science of Synchronicity and How Your Choices Shape Your World.* Berkeley: North Atlantic Books, 2019.

Nguyen, Dan. "Don't Forget: The Plural of Anecdote Is Data." Dan Nguyen's blog, Sept. 10, 2015, which references Nelson W. Polsby, *Political Science* 17, no. 4 (Autumn, 1984), p. 779.

Noone, Peter A. "The Holmes–Rahe Stress Inventory." *Occupational Medicine* 67, no. 7 (October 2017): 581–82.

Obama White House. "Behind the Lens: When the President Heard the News of the Supreme Court Decision on the Affordable Care Act." *Medium,* June 26, 2015.

Ockham, William. "The Noosphere (Part I): Teilhard de Chardin's Vision." Teilhard de Chardin website, August 13, 2013.

Ogburn, William F., and Dorothy Thomas. "Are Inventions Inevitable? A Note on Social Evolution." *Political Science Quarterly* 37, no. 1 (March 1922): 83–98.

Palmer, John. "The Challenge of Experimenter." *European Journal of Parapsychology* 13 (1997): 110–25.

Paskin, Willa. "Elizabeth Gilbert's 'Big Magic.'" *New York Times,* September 16, 2015.

Perry, Robert. *Signs: A New Approach to Coincidence, Synchronicity, Guidance, Life Purpose, and God's Plan.* Sedona, Ariz.: Semeion Press, 2009.

Playfair, Guy. *Twin Telepathy.* UK: White Crow Books, 2012.

Plimmer, Martin, and Brian King. *Beyond Coincidence: Amazing Stories of Coincidence and the Mystery and Mathematics Behind Them*. New York: St. Martin's Press, 2006.

Powell, David. "Earth's Moon Destined to Disintegrate." Space website. January 22, 2007.

Prochaska, J. O., and C. C. DiClemente. "Stages and Processes of Self-Change of Smoking: Toward an Integrative Model of Change." *Journal of Consulting and Clinical Psychology* 51, no. 3 (1983): 390–95.

Purves, D., G. J. Augustine, and D. Fitzpatrick, et al., eds. "Types of Eye Movements and Their Functions." In *Neuroscience*. 2nd ed. Sunderland, Mass.: Sinauer Associates, 2001.

Rawlette, Sharon Hewitt. "Are Coincidences Signs from God?" Mysteries of Consciousness blog, *Psychology Today*, February 5, 2020.

———. "How Skeptics Misapply the Law of Very Large Numbers." Connecting with Coincidence blog, *Psychology Today*, Jul 16, 2019.

———. *The Source and Significance of Coincidences*. Sharon Hewitt Rawlette, 2019.

Reefschläger, G. "Synchronizität in der Psychotherapie; Eine quantitativ-qualitative Untersuchung der strukturellen Beschaffenheit synchronistischer Phänomene im psychotherapeutischen Prozess," [Dissertation: Synchronicity in Psychotherapy] (2018). Frankfurt/Oder: Europa-Universität Viadrina Frankfurt, Kulturwissenschaftliche Fakultät.

Rickles, D., P. Hawe, and A. Shiell. "A Simple Guide to Chaos and Complexity." *Journal of Epidemiology and Community Health* 61, no. 11 (2007) 933–37.

Roberts, Sam. "Herman Rosenblat, 85, Dies; Made Up Holocaust Love Story." *New York Times*, February 21, 2015.

Roesler, C., and G. I. Reefschläger. "Jungian Psychotherapy, Spirituality, and Synchronicity: Theory, Applications, and Evidence Base." *Psychotherapy*. Advance online publication version, 2021.

Roxburgh, E. C., S. Ridgway, and C. A. Roe. "Issue 2: The Use of Qualitative Research in Developing Users' and Providers' Perspectives in the Psychological Therapies." *European Journal of Psychotherapy and Counselling* 17 (2015): 144–61.

Rushnell, SQuire. "Godwinks History page," *Godwinks* books on Godwinks website.

———. *When God Winks on Love*. New York: Atria Books, 2004.

Sacco, Robert G. "Dynamical and Statistical Modeling of Synchronicity: A

Probabilistic Forecasting Framework." *International Journal of Brain and Cognitive Sciences* 9, no. 1 (June 2020): 16–24.

———. "Fibonacci Harmonics: A New Mathematical Model of Synchronicity." *Applied Mathematics* 9, no. 6 (June 2018).

Scharf, Caleb A. "The Solar Eclipse Coincidence." *Scientific American,* May 18, 2012.

Schwartz, Gary. *Super Synchronicity: Where Science Meets Spirit.* Vancouver, BC: Param Media, 2017.

Schwarz, B. E. "Possible Telesomatic Reactions." *Journal of the Medical Society of New Jersey* 64 (1967): 600–603.

Science Buddies. "Probability and the Birthday Paradox." *Scientific American,* March 29, 2012.

Sheldrake, Rupert, and Pamela Smart. "Experimental Tests for Telephone Telepathy." *Journal of the Society for Psychical Research* 67 (July 2003): 184–99.

Shepherd, H. E. "The History of Coincide and Coincidence." *American Journal of Philology,* no. 3 (1880): 271–80.

Shermer, Michael. "Anomalous Events That Can Shake One's Skepticism to the Core." *Scientific American,* October 1, 2014.

———. "Do Anomalies Prove the Existence of God?" Michael Shermer website, May 12, 2018.

Silverman, Samuel. "Correspondences and Thought-Transference During Psychoanalysis." *Journal of American Academy of Psychoanalysis* 16, no. 3 (1988): 269–94.

Singer, Michael. *The Surrender Experiment.* New York: Harmony, 2015.

Sire, James W. *Discipleship of the Mind.* Madison, Wisc.: Intervarsity Press, 1990.

Small, Gary. "The Formula for Successful." *TEDx Talks,* January 30, 2018. YouTube.

Smith, Malcolm. "Why Is the Moon Exactly the Same Apparent Size from Earth as the Sun? Surely This Cannot Be just Coincidence; The Odds Against Such a Perfect Match Are Enormous." *Astronomy,* October 1, 2000.

Smurzyńska, Adrianna. "The Role of Emotions in Delusion Formation." *Studies in Logic, Grammar and Rhetoric* 48, no. 61 (2016).

Spacek, Sissy. *My Ordinary, Extraordinary Life.* New York: Hyperion, 2012.

Sparks, Gary J. "Study Guide for Marie-Louise Von Franz's Number and Time." J. Gary Sparks website.

Stanford, Rex G., and Angela Stio. "Associative Mediation in Psi-Mediated Instrumental Response (PMIR)." In *Research in Parapsychology 1975,* edited by J. D. Morris, W. G. Roll, and R. L. Morris. Metuchen, N.J.: Scarecrow Press, 1976.

Stanford, Rex G., R. Zennhausern, A. Taylor, and M. Dwyer, "Psychokinesis as a Psi-Mediated Instrumental Response." *Journal of the American Society for Psychical Research* 69 (1975): 127–33.

Stenger, Victor. *Quantum Gods: Creation, Chaos, and the Search for Cosmic Consciousness.* Amherst, N.Y.: Prometheus, 2009.

Stevenson, Ian. "Precognition of Disasters." *Journal of the American Society for Psychical Research* 64 (1970): 187–210.

———. *Telepathic Impressions.* New York: American Society for Psychical Research, 1970.

Stockbridge, Germaine, and Robin Wooffitt. "Coincidence by Design." *Qualitative Research* (2018): 1–18.

Storey, A. E., C. J. Walsh, R. L. Quinton, and K. E. Wynne-Edwards. "Hormonal Correlates of Paternal Responsiveness in New and Expectant Fathers." *Evolution and Human Behavior* 21, no. 2 (2000): 79–95.

"Strange Coincidences or Destiny Beyond Chance?" Richard Gardner. August 10, 2016, Youtube.

Swain, Frank. "How Do We Go Palm Oil Free?" *BBC Future,* January 13, 2020.

"Synchro Summit at Yale." Synchro Summit, Yale Divinity School, October 15–20, 2010.

Targ, E. "Evaluating Distant Healing: A Research Review." *Alternative Therapies in Health & Medicine* 3, no. 6 (1997): 74–78.

Tarnas, Richard. *Cosmos and Psyche.* New York: Penguin, 2006.

Todeschi, Kevin J. "Edgar Cayce on the Akashic Record." Edgar Cayce's A.R.E. website.

Townley, John, and Robert Schmidt. "Paul Kammerer and the Law of Seriality." In *Fortean Studies,* 251–60. London: John Brown, 1994.

Van Andel, Pek. "Anatomy of the Unsought Finding. Serendipity: Origin, History, Domains, Traditions, Appearances, Patterns and Programmability." *British Journal for the Philosophy of Science* 45, no. 2 (June 1994): 631–48.

Van Elk, M., K. Friston, and H. Bekkering. "The Experience of Coincidence: An Integrated Psychological and Neurocognitive Perspective." In *The Challenge of Chance,* edited by Klass Landsman and Ellen van Wolde. Springer, 2016.

Weaver, Warren. *Lady Luck: Theory of Probability.* New York: Anchor Books, 1963.

Williams, Gibbs. *Demystifying Meaningful Coincidences (Synchronicities): The Evolving Self, the Personal Unconscious, and the Creative Process.* New York: Jason Aronson, 2010.

Wimmer, Gary L. *A Second in Eternity.* Austin, Tex.: Lithomancy Institute, 2011.

Wise, Jeff. "When Fear Makes Us Superhuman." *Scientific American,* December 28, 2009.

Wood, Matt. "Neuroscience Researchers Receive $3.4 Million NIH Grant to Develop Brain-Controlled Prosthetic Limbs." *UChicago Medicine,* October 15, 2018.

WorldTribune Staff, "Coincidence? Simultaneous Power Outages Give Credence to Cyber-Doomsday Scenarios." *World Tribune,* April 23, 2017.

Wright, G. N., L. D. Phillips, P. C. Whalley, G. T. Choo, K. Ng, I. Tan, et al. "Cultural Differences in Probabilistic Thinking." *Journal of Cross-Cultural Psychology* 9, no. 3 (1978): 285–99.

Zylstra, Mathew. "Moments That Matter," Eyes4Earth website, October 24, 2017.

Index